First published in Great Britain in 2013 by Unkant Publishing,
First Floor Offices, Hoxton Point, 6 Rufus Street, London N1 6PE

Copyright © Ken Fox 2013

The right of Ken Fox to be identified as the author of this work has been asserted in accordance with the Copyright, Designs and Patents Act 1998.

Designed by Keith Fisher and Andy Wilson
Cover design by Andy Wilson

British Library Cataloguing-in-Publication Data

A CIP catalogue record for this book is available from the British Library
A Paperback Original

ISBN 978-0-9568176-4-8
1 3 5 7 9 10 8 6 4 2

All rights reserved. No part of this publication may be reproduced, stored in a retrieval system, or transmitted in any form or by any means without the prior permission of the publisher, nor be otherwise circulated in a binding or cover other than that in which it is published and without a similar condition being imposed on the subsequent purchaser.

Set in Unkant Jensen
www.unkant.com

AZMUD
AN OILY SAGA ON THE SURFACE OF THE WORDBATH IN 5 EXPIRED GENERATIONS

KEN FOX

Unkant Publishers
London

Ken Fox

Ken Fox lives and writes in Regina, Canada. From 1996 to 1998 he worked in the South Saskatchewan oil field, conducting environmental tests of drilling mud and sampling subsoil, an experience that informs much of his writing practice. Ken likes to write stuff that smells, and sometimes even looks, like poetry and has published 13 chapbooks of such verbal waste-matter. In 2010 he and life-partner Aleks McHugh co-published *Utilitarian Donuts*. He is the host & programmer of *Naval Aviation In Audio* on CJTR Regina Community Radio. Favourite quotes include *"Let's all be prophets!"* (Moses) and *"Let's all be composers!"* (Zappa).

Introduction	ix
MIAZMUD	5
ZOON'S YLIAD	65
ELAZMUD, THE WRECKING	113
ZEEN'S AYNED	125
THE FRICTION HORSES	*127*
THE PROTOZOANS	*146*
THE OZONE ELEVATOR	*173*
ACTIVATED SLUDGE	*187*
VOYAGE OF THE PLAZMUD	*197*

INTRODUCTION

The price of admission here is not knowing what's going on, although we all know what's going on: a glass front on the blood-spattered workhouse offering smoothie cocktails with guilty tonsils at the end of the straw. I mean, really! In belaboured knowingness, the same thing at every station bookstall: narcissism, celebrity codswallop, feelgood greens and all that phony stuff on DIY and sports. Where 'free radical expression' has become a name for the purest spiel-to-the-funders drivel on careening autodrive, a recent replacement for the scrotum-tightening clichés 'genre transgression' and 'breaks all boundaries'. But, personally, my taut, brittle and expectant hymen requires something more potent in the tackle department! *Here it is*, ladies and gentlemen, and if you can't understand it, it's because you're too involved with some decadent scam to know what blowing your nose sounds like. The secret name of Ken Fox's *Azmud*, prompted

---

NB. Certain of these ideas were first worked out in an edition of Ben Watson's radio show *Late Lunch With Out To Lunch* called 'Integrity as String-on-Vest' on Resonance FM on 4 April 2007. It may be heard at *archive.org/details/IntegrityAsString-on-vestLate4-iv-2007*. For some reason there's a compressed performance of John Cage's 4'33" at the start, Out To Lunch starts at approximately 1:55.

by recent moral turbitudes refluxing in the dark waters of the esemplastic psyche, is 'Integrity as String-on-Vest'.

If we are going to talk noise, let's talk *Naval Aviation in Audio*, Ken Fox's weekly show on Regina Community Radio (CJTR), where punk and metal fight it out with the best that 'literature' has to offer. High time for such raw and vital monsters to rise up from the forgotten whirls of punk history and gob at current art imposture, whose brocaded address to the nation's lovers of fine music is a skimpy designer patch on the streetbroken actuality. In alchemical retort, overworked curses brewed from the plan-man kitchen designate a postulate which breaks apart those affected [Aphex] twins of history: what's said and what happened. That scandalous gap which founds your bakery, snoot pants. And the dislocation Ken Fox's lingo works on your growing onions knows no unison with the solvent airs of your nice grease, your self-serving nonchalance about the arbitrary: this broken toss is not arbitrary, man, it's *motivated*, even if the tensions spring–*boinnng!*–from no cultural tradition you can trace. It springs from the senses, man. Planet Five Star. With umbrage by the grockle pub, where only a thousand-year-old baked potato smothered in some disgraceful topping can assuage your lust for dust and acrimony. *Noise, noise, noise?* What is this weak, second-hand fart reeking through the current art propaganda? Just remember: no-one can say anything remotely serious about 1968 who hasn't experienced Tommy James and the Shondells. Their 'Hanky Panky' concentrates such a manifest of pertinent and pressing themes, it threatens to explode like a super-nova. In this, it's just like *Azmud*.

"*The poet works with mental ears. Via this specialized audition the real-time sounds of speech and vocalized utterance are disintegrated into sub-lexical acoustic noise by analogy with the striking clatter of real work in the material world. Plus also bird-song, weather sounds, and the cognates.*" (J.H. Prynne,

'Mental Ears and Poetic Work', *Chicago Review*, 2009 p. 128). Of course, this is *alchemy*, with its injunction to pulverize, precipitate, purify and volatilize. But it's also our own material relationship to the external world, as we bite, chew and digest its bits and pieces to provide the building blocks of our bodies and the ATP to power our muscles and nerves. Prynne calls this action on the elements 'poetry', but it's in fact what we all do everyday. If they have a function to perform, poets and their poetry wake us up to these material transactions.

Music like that of Oliver Nelson in 1961, sturdy and inventive, capable of sustaining the most stringent musical and sociological investigations, remains the standard and model by which all aspects of the contemporary wack must be examined, judged and disposed of. Unfortunately, *objective analysis of the social causes of aesthetic not-up-to-scratchness* tends to produce instant indigestion on the part of artists, especially those who feel they've sacrificed lucrative careers in stockbroking or merchant-banking to heroically pursue lives in art. Actually, to be an artist is to fail in the realm of spectacular values, and I seriously mean *fail*, all the way to weeping as you return home from job interviews. That's where Ken Fox writes from.

Tottering fop David Kusworth demonstrates that looking and living like Johnny Thunders enables you to play music which doesn't sound like the kind of calculated, squeaky-clean simulacrum of past glories which serves as the usual commercial-rock recipe today (and that includes all this art-rock rubbish I keep tripping over). Failure is the magic dust which enables a host of misfits and geniuses on disability benefit to outdo the crimes of Brit Art all day and every day. Which is why mental-health bureaucrat John Wilkinson, living on the other side of the fence, can be fired by the best of intentions and the most graded literary inputs, but remains stolidly incapable of writing an affecting poem. Given this fact, it's a little upsetting to read in a recent book of interviews with poets (edited by Tim Allen and Andrew Duncan for Salt, and called *Don't Start Me Talking*) that Sean Bonney, currently my favourite word-mangler, remains so under the cosh of identity politics he thinks that, *"as a well educated white male he could go and make a lot of money working for a merchant bank, or something"* (DSMT, p. 53). But he chooses not to. Perhaps Bonney was being funny—as Frank Zappa once observed, irony in interviews doesn't usually work in print—but even so, the extent of personal delusion here is disturbing. I'm afraid Lloyds wouldn't touch you with a bargepole, Sean, even if you started ironing your shirts and reading the *Telegraph*! You've got David Kusworth's indelible incense on your clothes, man, whether you like it or not.

Poetry is objective, not ethical. In this regard, let's hear from **Benedetto Croce**:

— a warm and vivid consciousness of the real nature of poetry in its original function: ... this miracle was worked by the keen, restless and stormy mind of **Giambattista Vico**.

He criticised at once the three doctrines of poetry as a means of adorning and communicating intellectual truth, as merely subservient to pleasure, and as a harmless mental exercise for those who can do it. Poetry is not esoteric wisdom: it does not presuppose the logic of the intellect: it does not contain philosophical judgments. The philosophers, in finding these things in poetry, have simply put them there themselves without realising it. Poetry is produced not by the mere caprice of pleasure, but by natural necessity. It is so far from being superfluous and capable of elimination, that without it thought cannot arise: it is the primary activity of the human mind. Man, before he has arrived at the stage of forming universals, forms imaginary ideas. Before he reflects with a clear mind, he apprehends with faculties confused and disturbed: before he can articulate, he sings: before speaking in prose, he speaks in verse: before using technical terms, he uses metaphors, and the metaphorical use of words is as natural to him as that which we call "natural." So far from being a fashion of expounding metaphysics poetry is distinct from and opposed to metaphysics. The one frees the intellect from the senses, the other submerges and overwhelms it in them: the one reaches perfection in proportion as it rises to universality, the other, as it confines itself to the particular: the one enfeebles the imagination, the other strengthens it. The one takes precautions against turning the mind into body, the other delights in giving body to mind. The judgments of poetry are composed of reflection, which if introduced into poetry makes it frigid and unreal: and no one in the whole course of history has ever been at once a great poet and a great metaphysician [N.B. overleaping this barrier is what Marx achieved in *Capital*–and what the AMM is trying to do today]. *Poets and philosophers may be called respectively the senses and the intellect of mankind: and in this sense we may retain as true the scholastic saying* "there is nothing in the intellect which was not first in the senses." *Without sense, we cannot have intellect: without poetry, we cannot have philosophy, nor indeed any civilisation.*

That was Giambattista Vico's account of poetry from his *Scienza Nuova* of 1725, as expounded by Benedetto Croce in 1910, and translated into English three years later (*The Philosophy of Giambattista Vico*, London: Howard Latimer, 1913, pp. 48-49) by **R.G. Collingwood**, the great historical idealist who lost the battle over British philosophy in the 1940s; the victory went to Logical Positivism, condemning British philosophy to intellectual bankruptcy and cultural irrelevance for the rest of the century (a slough of despond unrelieved by the influx of Continental philosophy over the last three decades). It's not that everyone should engage in the somewhat diminished and impotent practice we presently call 'writing poems'. Vico's definition of poetry is exalted and starry, it concerns knowledge and nature and society, the dizzy heights of thinking about thought itself. Vico and Croce use the word 'poetry' to describe an initial response to the world without which all reasoning is vain; other critics of bourgeois positivism have used different terms—Marx's 'dialectic'; Freud's 'unconscious'; Benjamin's 'intoxication'; Adorno's 'fantasy'—but they all hurled their accusations at the same target. All attacked the bourgeois assumption that positive science is the only real form of knowledge. They had good reason. Modern science has indeed become a set of pragmatic disciplines bent on supplying techniques for capitalist exploitation, completely sundered from the holistic idea of knowledge implied by the word 'science' in Classical and Renaissance times. Even to those sceptical about Marx and Freud, it's evident that the victory of 'scientific thought' has not produced a reasonable world, in fact quite the opposite—war, mass starvation, child slavery and climate change are just four topics the mass media seem to find unavoidable.

Positivism did not rise unchallenged. René Descartes, who formulated the metaphysic which today underlies both commonsense and post-structuralist radicalism, did not have it all his own way. In the eighteenth century, Vico, along with **Hermann Samuel Reimarus**, the theorist of animal art instincts based in Hamburg, inveighed against him. Vico anticipated the damage Descartes' famous championing of mathematics over history would do to both knowledge and society. Think about it. Each time a natural ecosystem or functioning human community is destroyed by capitalist enterprise, we witness mathematics—the assessment of profit and loss according to economic criteria, i.e. sheer number—bulldoze traditions, requirements and aspirations any responsible historical understanding would honour. As Marx said in a footnote to *Capital*, Vico recognised that human beings, not gods or heroes or ideas, make history—an insight that still sounds critical and unorthodox today.

But why Vico now? Because if poetry is a word for our *first psychic grapple with the external world*, the initial images and cadences and urges without which all definitions and measurements and numbers would be meaningless, then poetry is *objective*, not *ethical*; an actuality, not an ought-to-be. Ever-present, not an add-on: an ongoing, ubiquitous process happening in every mind beneath the whirring cogs of reason; a dream dreamt by everyone, not a cultural bonus available to the few. I grant that such a point of view will not be popular in artistic circles, where those who 'maintain the fiction' are hoisted high on the shoulders of the grant-hungry art mob (hello Brian Eno, Kaffe Matthews, Mats Lindström). By 'maintaining the fiction', I mean the activities of those promo-artistes and ad-copy writers who claim that art is good for us, it brings us together, makes us less racist and sexist and generally obnoxious. However, the notion of culture civilising a savage population is the *purest conservative humbug*. It was developed during the nineteenth century versus working-class demands for the vote. In this argument, 'culture' really means *property*. Property-owners are terrified by those without property, even as they exploit them for cheap labour and fleece them with high rents. Matthew Arnold's concept of culture as 'sweetness and light' which soothes the savage breast is simply the property-owner desperate for the poor to share his values—without resisting his extraction of surplus value. You can find the idea of top-down 'mollification' in **Samuel Taylor Coleridge**, and it's there in R.G. Collingwood—unlike his critique of Logical Positivism, his *The New Leviathan* is the purest statement of political conservatism. This was also the argument used in apartheid South Africa to explain why Blacks did not have the vote—they weren't yet 'civilised' enough to deserve it. Weirdly enough, all kinds of oh-so-radical artists use the same argument when they apply for grants—the population is benighted, consumes cultural garbage, some righteous funded artwork will make them 'see anew' and 'challenge their preconceptions'—as if *capitalism-as-usual* isn't supplying us with monstrosities which 'challenge our preconceptions' every day!

Okay, if the top-down idea of enlightenment is patronising and conservative, what is this arcane stuff Unkant insists on publishing to place on your most prized domestic bookshelf next to Trotskyist accounts of World War II and scurrilous critiques of Tony Cliff's 'Leninism'? Why do we do it, and what's the fuss about? Well, to refer back to Vico, the poetic culture we broadcast is the *"primary activity of the human mind"*, your favourite and dominant mediations broken into and transformed into immediate pleasures, patterns, rhythms and buffoonery. Vico watched the gradual desanctification of modern life with some bemusement: as Gods became metaphors and finally abstractions to be thrown about in conversation, as heroes became butts of jokes and names of streets and banks, he noticed that something flawed the new democracy. The degradation of divine metaphor to an everyday token—Britannia on the banknote—means that the intellect overawes the imagination. People's psychic investment in the game wilts. Then society entered a new period of barbarism, which he called the *ricorso* (Collingwood's translation is 'reflux'), in which everything became muddled up again, until a new divine age emerged, but one preserving and transforming what had happened previously. James Joyce's *Finnegans Wake* was based on Vico's *Scienza Nuova* just as his *Ulysses* was based on *The Odyssey*: what he meant by the polyglot inscrutability of Finnegans Wake was *ricorso*, a smashing-up and parody of languages of learning and rhetorics of power, so that a new vitality could emerge, in which word and thing-described were connected again. That's what Ken Fox is doing in *Azmud*. This stuff won't rest on the page, flattering the sophisticated readers who've learned to stop their lips moving as they read. It screams to be READ ALOUD, to be shouted from balconies, performed down telephones and frothed and fumed during demos, occupations and riots. And *that's* why we like it so much.

Out To Lunch
Somers Town
11-i-2013

DEDICATION

for Aleks
the vector
in my apple-core

&

Shania
the atom-masher
in my play-stem

ENTERDUCTORY UNKANTATION

UP

all, air, amplify,
azmuth, extract, always ox
execute...

NORTH

when nuth's affront & locks unlip & fonts flow froth like sky-green gob goes gray goes math goes mosh. All over the time mind gathers turbulent sludge gets barrage gets a sniff of nother nuff. If there's not a nuff then stuff it with nuth? ho no! out of noth, th'on grows.

WEST

while well-dressed ghosts get wasted on sewage & rotstew & thereoff bester at blessings blasted nod off notes at faltering wet-jets, or yet when outstreaming wendsdays mold up piling mud on mud & walk on walk of thickening middles & what drowns the lastlight off horse-battered bonanza.

EAST

even if eventual airthing ends evening up momentous earth-ark, dearth of air come dirt of earth, even airthic amplitude ears open up events worth eating, even teaweed eden in airseat invents rising reasons for test-tasting adjective outthrow or jetjam or eggwaste.

SOUTH

wherever in the outbeaming sum there is a sumth in-swimming in mormud, where thick mor bobs upon compiling dead-ponds or of underall pokes up whole sums spoofing sumtings odd of sumppits pumping off unwanted floodstuff, comes soth comes tosh comes tush comes shut comes shot comes shout.

DOWN

now under oxecution's onerous void,
do, do, do, do…

MIAZMUD

A GAS NOVEL

OPENING MONOMOUTH

ICTUS, RAPTUS, CAPTUM, SPAZUM. A stroke, a blow, a thrust of voices. Apoplectic fulmination. Potent portent peril pervading.

What a we are we, is I, is this, this it, this machine, it, I, I, as mud we'd work as one would weed a sea-shelf of recycling book pulp, pumping back to fibrous pregnation all plasmic-basket interior potential & even tore a bit off the Oily Bubble. But what a word! What a unwood burnworld we escaped to bathe & breath in, out, this gas-fuelled ark-engine rasping up what lucky ore-strikes, ox-hoards, lumps of dung spun out of the living lung. In chunks, it comes, in caskets, we gather under another tax break attack & Regina spills its coffins.

Create a setting. A gaseous habitat, a bright grey opacity, a captum spazum, sonic manifestation of global inflation, a whisper, a word, a human herd cutting thru noxious turbulent gamble. To live in this is to live a lie, yet notwithstanding blind groping & broken hoses & amplified dosage, we persist, dragging about our malfunctioning ark-engine-artifactory, leaving this inflated vapour tale, leaving this ripe wakage to plume thru the metaphysical turbidity.

A Plot? A plan, a patch of ground to sink in. Ictus raptus, to roll into a ball the structure of interrelated irreversible action with a sense of causality & plop *that* into the pansubstantial toxic pond? Into the pan then! Panic! Attack! Panoramic landfill, industrial lunch, full-emersion schematic baptism, lagoon of cosmic sewage, basketsful of overvoided mutter...

How fatal, how novel.

Into that *ictus pozum*, this must happen: 150 filled by nite. A full one-fifty before the embers die. And a site opens already full of holes & blank stones. Nevertheless, our motivator exists, expends, invests his self in desert-crawling us: he paid us, he made us. We seize our

Our prime mover for conversion of trapped spirit into locomotored matter & propulsion of ships both merchant & naval.

breezy covenant, heave our empty chest & say *nabum grabum snuffum stuffum!*

Sequestered in adject oblivion captus, shot froth from ruptus gas novel (the burst nozzle of our sagging navel), confiscated nostrils digging under tumultuous puddle, the power to synthesize squandered, we keep the purest spazum free from the fire, fearing formal dissolution, toxic release, loss of function ... but to know those strange strings by so many names & to have come so far just to get a toxic whiff ...

BREATHING EXERCISE No.1

VACCUUMS TO THE SKY, *mudsuckers! The diamonds won't just drop in our sacks like wads of spiked gauze in your infected ears! Start your engines, peasants! You are allowed. You hear me? You are* ALOUD.

 Aaaaaaaaaaa–laaaaaaaaaa–ooooooooo-dd.
 Aaaaaaaaaaa–laaaaaaaaaa–ooooooooo-dd.
 Aaaaaaaaaaa–laaaaaaaaaa–ooooooooo-dd.
 Aaaaaaaaaaa–laaaaaaaaaa–ooooooooo-dd.
 Aaaaa-laaaa-oooo-d. Aaaaa-laaaa-oooo-d.
 Aaaaa-laaaa-oooo-d. Aaaaa-laaaa-oooo-d.
 Ala-owed, ala-owed, ala-owed, ala-owed.

Aloud! (allowed). Aloud! (allowed). You are aloud!–you are allowed–you are aloud!–you are allowed–you are aloud!–you are allowed–you are aloud–you are allowed!

EMISSION STATEMENT UNFOLDS, WITH EMENDMENTS

THUS NOURISHED, THUS MOTIVATED, crunching thru bonified particulate tempest, gas meters running.
  A source, a site...

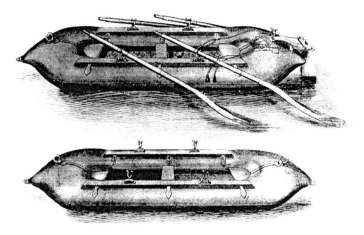

Draft of a raft, a drift into the past, copy to front & check back for passages lacking: In the beginning there was only Word... & paste in the current.

We clean the area completely, auger in, press our patch over the punctured surf, pray for thirty seconds & inflate. But what cuts the rubber hull? What breaches this manic inflation? What artificial industry sabotages our manual fracture?

Strike the nervous edge with your quivering inkpen. We drink, we sink, we think, at end beheading the unneeded prefixing from its freed fuel. Knees quick in the spillage, bodily knobs coming swim-ready with laborious grease.

A yarn to earn an hour or a yearn to burn a year, all ears turn further up the bloated azmouth to capture what it, us, we, I, it, this machine, spins worthy wealth collecting, to stash
 in a fractured artfact scrapped from epic lab, a crate we drag or chest we heave as smoke we float as coal aghast a blast of crust across the atom-packed horizons.

TICTUS INDESPIZUM, RAPTUS INDESPAZUM. *A band of temple robbers looking for loot in a strange land are not among the standard mythologic characters & sacred laws or exegetic traditions on the purifaction of the sacreligious are unattested*, says Arc Parker, our on-board expert in air pollution. He parked his arc upon a hive & now he's an epicademical star (or was that a car on a rack or a rat caught in tar? Don't even get it started!)

Nevertheless, beyond the schematic borders, here is us, it, I, I, this we, perspiring to cross the sacred hedges, surrounded by interdiction, to cross the winter inhibition, cutting thru the antidiction, creeping under prohibition to break the crapping exhibition! Inhibition, interdiction, exhibition, extradiction, prohibition, protodiction, abhibition, abolition! Picked us, ripped us, wrapped us in spatum,
 to blast barred, bombed, into the scarred crust, out of habit, under bombardment, squatting in enemy position, airwaves sterilized with deathly sonic onion, unarmed, unplugged, cut from function, cut from production, is us, is we, this I, this it, this mechanical artifact dumping in front of the inflammatory bankage, an untouchable spring, things unspoken, is us, this we, this wheeling mobile factory, abstracting into the unentered spaces. All to fill the General's cold coffers!

To get inside the visionary spaces & occupy the prophetic places. To rip a scripture from its raps & leave a gift on its blanked-out pages.

Is there real danger? Even under the warmest days, in the sanctity of an unsullied meadow lay stacks of untouched objects that may be inserted in our ark-engine & ignited to disturb the ritual dreaming – dare we?

You want to drift into the olfactory stages & sniff your waste thru the stinky traces? Strip a structure from its straps & build contraptions with its parts? The only danger you're in is the fumes from your malfunctioning back-ass vac-truck. But still the stink is all about you & the danger opaque & omnipresent! So says a passing chorus of vagrant trash babies coasting thru the ad-vents.

So slaves on a rank airship we stink with our working wage & wither in whether or not to eat winter wind or live without shiver. Shit, with quicksilvers sinking in we live in our taxing skins, tanning hides & heads invisible. Does it dissolve in the bloodstream, this fragile parasitic branch? It knows us & grows us & gets in us & grows in us & we in it but we don't ever even get to meet it.

We build our nitely ark to raid the sacred spaces & lay our eggs in prophetic places, & all along the way we say *hey vagrant trash babies what about a ride in the reeds?* Some come, most blow on.

To inflate the ineffible relics with flatulent exultations, to fill the hungered filthy rubber crates with oddball exhalations. Hoho – hahah! Hoho – hahah! Inflated mattress modifies to raft, overinflation tantamounts to flattery, over-mountainous mess reverts to flatness, unpumped paradise deflates to bedrock. Hoho – hahah! Hoho – hahah! Hoho – hm-hmmm. Hoho – hm-hmmm.

So it goes.

A DOSE

AROMATIC INFLUX of hard current, excess adiabatic export, bank picnic underpinned by mopping policy. Soak up repo options & bond the billowing billions in their rallies. Cut key rates with aggressive increase. Drain the liquid remains.

Inflocks the worldly-bird dropping white coin disturb onto placid air-hole, turbulating thru rapid-galactic talk-walls as income is downstream thump & flutter after brass hornblasts bloat arid engine to open exit chutes but before analog infusions invade electric compound.

Acrobatic influff of drab correction, abscess ambient inland port plunks banked birdseed deeply with ramming updraft. Sponge down pop-up opinions & adhere to baloney-baked bully-cheese thru breezy pipeline. Molt cramped lock-star with diagrammatic plastic heave & collect in downdressed windbasket the blessed drains. A sample administered anaerobically, unexemplary.

AN EPISODE

ORE AS EPIC as any other patch of pierced sod we suppose.

An industrial compound. All the herms were monumentally mutilated, infested cracks recreating every inward aspect of the quadrilateral tapered shaft.

And on our craft we held high our severed head, bearing the broken bust of our illegal lunch like so much bagging luggage as we attached our tubes to the loose pharynx.

But at that exact instant the aforementioned Arc Parker, a qualified on-board scripter, intoned a prophetic sequence that mutilated our outbound schematic & smelled out a bad omen for the voyage: *igduz rabidus gabidum subidum — the 150 must never be filled!* he inchanted in his chains, knees rattling, *The topped-up tanks will not mean merely quotational satisfaction, the full fuel-fill will fail, spell total destruction, the end of the onion-run & the ruin of air-one!*

Oh Dear! Oh Dire! How dare we, how will we ever fulfill our sacred compilation with such evil omens fulfilling our daily noses?

But we're nothing if we ever forget our only function, the very submission of our existence, is air-ore extraction. So we invoke a sack of sacred equipment & begin blasting up again.

BUBBLES OUT

DART OF DEATH is wealth of dearth. Thru the vector sink the soils with manufractured matter's exterior magnitude & intense traction, against tradition, landfull filled with arid circus. But of what 150 bubbles does it blow? How to mold a map or fold a puddle into a global muddle?

Ictus, picktus, postum, mostum. Flat is floor & flatter is repeated patter with the flat of a hand to pump up the head of rubber or flat falters unpumped where flattery rather inflates.

And our collision waiver does not cover towing where terms are violated or undercarriage damage in collisions caused by underclearance even if deflationary reaction relieves pressure.

Talking to trash-babies with canned snacks to increase amplitude. Trash babies in ad-plazma spitting up the excess of their venal invections. Ruptum sputum.

A wheel in print, a rash tread of texture

Amplitude melts into sonic sea-waves, something something thrashing trash in adjective flotsamic body, splash in the unwashed regions.

Blame the nerve centre, BLAM BLAM, blame the monastic monopoles, BLOOM BLOOM, but anyway you blow it, it inflates, expands, not into emptiness, Zerox, oil-taster, gas-sniffer, asphalt-tester, insists, but into nothingness, there are no empty vessels to fill, it insists, the 150 are already full & always were. The fact of the blow-out is the elazmic rubbermatter, not the illusory vacancy within, internal bendum, stretchum, spandum.

Of course, this wretched robbermutter heresy has been reported to the total formal tribunal, whose current constipatory caseload is backed up to well before the BIG BANG BOOM.

MANUFACTURED BREATH?

DENIASNES of the well-bonified prophets takes his samples into his mobile epical lab, knowing full well the wind in his preverbial sales was always inspiration, the breath of life, the gust of which he guesses is perhaps actual breath, hoho–hm-hmmm, hoho–hm-hmmm, gaseous atmos, aeros, aria, the stuff that animates with toxic spirit the corporeal earthly vessel, which his nose now knows is a cargo ship named the Plazmud, the soul purpose of which he hears is to transport ore from ear to air to eventual earth,

   hoho–hahah! hoho–hahah!

The question then, he says, *is in an age of industry how does one synthesize those spirits, generate those gusts in a place where whole oceans are stuffed in intertrinkling databanks & ships burn lifesauce to fund their epic crawl?* He turns a tap, opens a valve & the conditioned atoms turns toxic in their spheres…

   hehe! hehe! hehe! oooooooooohhh!

A band of temple robbers looking for loot in a strange land are not among the standard mythologic characters

ON DESERT SURVIVAL

THE VERY AIR IS RICH WITH ORE, the active ingredient of which is a real ox of a horse to harness. We measure the dosage with a little extra in this instance & shake down with all radios active & brought upon ourcells, the perpetrators of this most striking exception, a torrent of execration...

Ouch! Ark! It, this, this it, this I, is out, is ahh, is art! is all act, is outfront, is all in, is Ouch! Arf! It farts, is traffic, is car, on rack, scarred, on fire, no, don't go, please don't go up again.

Let it speak. It wants to talk to the fully bonified prophets who reside in the day-old bone-pile full-time.

But he, Arc Parker, parked again, farted up, & started his arcane carriage again, as shot messenger avenging, reminding that herald is courageous courier of faraway flavour, is clear specimen sample of indispensable function shrouded under uncondemned tabooular shield. Upright holy relic talking the walk.

And he, Parker again, squatting in his vacant spot again, also said the Phonecians amazed the Grecians by greasing up the phonic mazes & crossing the axle-impaled atlas to occupy the unprotected sonic deltas & perform their ritual access rights with the uploading of forbidden objects & every brand of bluddy afterbath ensued them.

Get the coded message? To protect ourcells we must download all his elaborate rituals, just to keep the deathbats out of our mindshafts.

Even so, it keeps doing. *Ictus raptus spatum trapsus.* Toxigen lungkiller erodes every function. Turbulent jets govern all prophetic craft. Putrifaction makes the metaphysical painful as fructal traffic makes the holy goat palpable. Fixed lustral bowls enliven revolting manholes. Purifying encirclements slice their sick dog to weld their split god. Invasive external incursions occur even under Athena's clock, where the principal public purification lays in unloosing her muddy scapeghost. Survival seems unfit for even the fittest destinations. Even if anyhow unfinished, all must end.

Must plan ever expand into actual action?

QUESTION AND ANSWER

WHAT THEN IS THE WIND's active agent?

A bigger blast, compressed, shredded, a dance embedded, pressed thru animate engines & amplified, distorted, corrected, embalmed, packaged, priced, shipped, purchased, expended, discarded, degraded, expired, hoarse voices scratching at the epic surface, electric whales thrashing about the pneumatic depths, breath basins abused by flailing trunks, all in tiny pools poured, all as saucers flown.

Or, more broadly speaking, an ounce, an inch, a spoken second, a muscular minute twitching thru its manufactured habit, feeding on channeled gas-fires, importing ox-power in hour-long slugs, becoming begetter of all things sharp & sour as diatomic scales grow on all our faces.

And this, this power, this do do action, your very own go-go juice, is the stuff they're after with their samplers & their shovels & their mud-drills & giant syringes & extractors & pump-jacks & mind-shafts & gold-pans & silver straws & flaming maws.

Now do you know why its ears always go OUCH even as its nose is all go, go, go?

AN OUNCE OF UTTERLY UNTRUE TESTIMONY AS TO OUR ORIGINARY COMMISSION

DRUNKEN, TARGUZZLING General Motors descended upon Zerox's asphalt testing lab & loomed about, flaunting his rank emission, fingering various samples,

& Zerox, Tartester, Stargrazer, Asphaltic Inventor, startled at the noxious presence, awaited instructions, which soon spilled out:

> I heard you've brewed a grade of tar with ox enough for one spoon to fuel a whole biomechanical herd a hundred years.
>
> Answered Zerox, it may be true, but further testing....
>
> Magnificent news. I will need 150 units fully fueled before year's end.
>
> Zerox faded. I am but a labman, a technician, I don't do, I can't do industrial scale.
>
> Demonspatum, Zerox. Get off your ass & make a plan. Get help, get loads, but do.
>
> But I am but a scientician, a tester, I don't do outbound contracts.
>
> Doubledemonspatum! Deploy a crew. Deploy your brother Zoon, who knows the field. Get out, get around, leave your cozy comfort tomb & be a man-ager!
>
> OK I'll see what I can do…
>
> Quadrupledemonspatum with a dozen dead angels stacked in a bloody heap!!! Fulfill my 150 before the end of the burning embers or I'll have you injected with the bestial fuels & see how many miles I can get out of you!

PRAGMANIC MONOLOG

WHAT WHAT WAD is this slice of individuated sausage off the long-stock, stack on a rack unstuck from global bondage? It is I, this, frail spazum, asmud, unstuck stock. I am uncut, occult, unclear, oblique.

Can walk, can walk word over word with sinking feet, frolicking, picnicking, panicking in heap. Can dream awake dread wages, can rip together digital package, sleep apart nebulous plastic creations stretched out of bituminous commune, can burn together fibrous masses, sick stock for evaluation, for flaunting at death-markets as life-song unsung but edible in ink-frame & derivable as format-transfer capital capture cumulous for custom spirit capacitor house-boat install.

Camera-ready verb-files proturbing thorough over pulp wilderness, this is occultic riddle filtered thru collective commercial time-transfer. I own up. I drop name. I gather rights. I hoist possession, this oracular oral cabbage decaying. I wrought in ink village. I collect in pulp mountain. I ascend holy commode, prosperous seeking grist for hungry engine.

Am absurd, as think-wad shaking. Am bonded, bound to, bounding from, rebounded to Wascana Creek, as earth transfer trickling. Am job office plunking as this, finger-linking component strapped to transfer apparatus & obliged to prime mover.

Give job now. Give it wages for work. Get you southbound & go up in the mountain & see what wealth therein dwells. Enter wired caves, evade plasma network, insert yourself into the center well & ascend.

What cities, what tents, what good bad trash therein? What fat seams, lean streaks? Be BOLD, bring first fruit you find therein.

Now is the time to mine the first grapes before the apocalyptic living creatures ever again are herded into their waste eating habit.

Go where the brook branches & cut pages with grape-clusters & bare it on a yoke. Return after 40 hours & speak of coal & gas & black shakes & yellow cake.

THE CURIOUS LEGEND OF OTTO'S CYCLE

OTTO NICKLESS, ENGINEER in our own rhyme, quit his office, ate & got gas. He evacuated his atomsphere & freed his favourite four pistons to ride the pock-lipped heavens spreading streaks of crazy fume in tiny curls across the besmudged constellations.

A volatile snail seen between the deathly throes of its thermodynamic autocycle

Otto's engine's action is a furious up-down stroke within a cylindrical cell. It turns the whales of fortune thru their economical spazums.

He checks his meters to ensure the needles are behaving, sits in his custom gas chamber, draws in rich coal thru his lead pipe, stands, compresses his wastepaper & makes pulpic mound, sits again, ignites his powerpiles with electric spark, & last, stands again in his chamber & exhausts his vapours in down-scaled articulate clouds.

He sees the epic shapes cast their spells upon the cloudy sheets, hears the pleasant hum of all his devices igniting & increases the pace of his audiovascular cycle – but then, in this instant, hears a hideous grind as his gears falter & halt. *Goddamn all mechanical devices & their digital superiors for a billion years!* he sneers.

What do you do in such sickening scenario? Do you allow your personal digits to tinker unprotected within the savage network? Do you load your ballistic lung & shoot up trouble? Do you pray to General Motors for sympathic recourse? Or do you do what Otto does?

You do. You unfold your manual & engage the angry monster, enter its labyrinth, seek to steal its habitual meal.

You take a sip of orange tonic, exercise your oxygating apparatus, allow the charged atoms to incite your particles, charge your blood electric, insert a capacitous pool into your secondary reactor to allow the charges to circulate thru the surround & manifest the lax miazmud.

First, make sure your jets are gestating in their nest. Descend thru the ether to the backside of the delinquent engine. The two ruling lights hang high above.

If the top light is green, the channels are open, if the light falters, the currents are haltered. If at the bottom a yellow light flashes, jam traffic is backing back into spectacular panic.

Shit! You realize the ether is vacant. You climb back into the gas chamber, find the entrance to the nest & shift the coloured threads into a favourable config, incite the engine to choke up a smoky scripture

& ingest...

Vapid! Voiceless! Vacuous! Voided! Suffocating you grasp at your flailing meter, break glass, grab the nearest needle, break off a random bubble-sheet & pop a few to inhale your tiny quotient of toxic spirit.

Alive, naked, asphyxiated, you crawl thru the arid maze, searching for little holes to suck on, any bit, any lick, any cubic inch of life not consumed by the surrounding apparatic madness.

You read, you consume & are consumed. You settle into smooth rapturous groove. You would like to invoke manual override, but your digits lack the necessary memory of primordial mechanical manipulation. Enslaved, you are Otto, entombed in corroded sonic scrypt & degrading.

End of legend.

A RANDOM TRASH BABY
TALKS INFLATIONARY SPACES

HEY TRASH BABY I see you got the hot wave & world fire all over, I see you got on your freaky weather.

Reach in now & show me the globe, reach into your godblog pocket & pull out an atom, world-grain, parcel of cold cold ocean.

I know, I know, you told it all on icy sheets, you blew the arctic increase, you consumed & blew out the news. But tell me again where you leaped, what your nervous skyhooks released.

Comes the listing reply, as a red whale riding a bloody microwave streak:

1. A vast rock broke off the interior cavity & navigated the ironic plasma channels into the capillary ranges & there must clog passage of gas cargo which must in result externally expand, jamming at last, bursting the conductive tissue.

2. See the hills retreat into their hells. See how the tumult doubles as the waving wollups trouble the coasting wells.

3. Or look at the spinning records, how they wax hot on their isolating ratios, spitting out gob after gob of bright orange & red, the drastic blast of alarms locked on, on, on, on, the streaming screaming tedium.

4. Loot the technocratic ocean, its steaming miazmal magmatudes, loot Noah's dead tongue as it leaks its last crumb of moist dust onto the glowing gaseous mountain, whose mechanical piles pulse with magypnotic muscle, pneumatic thoracies croaking up deathly inventions by the dozen.

Well I'll be godoubledamned if that's not a clue to our emission's folded feature!

THE WHOLE PICTURE IN FOG, IN MINIATURE

FROM THAT TO THIS, an ancient steam engine gasping glorified forces, a series of human hearts inciting wet flux thru flushing matrix, a baked brain-farm firing up charged symbols, dictating signals thru their myriaded secretarial pools, two homosapien spirits encased in superstitial tanks, heaving, heaving, heaving the weight of scriptures ripped from fossilized halos & found drifting out of manhole covers & descending from stratacasted fog-layers, taking the haloed passages inthru the orifice, thru the vestibule, down the wind rivers thru their branching to the converter stations & sending back the spliced life-dream to erupt somewhere above & befog the lab thru metamorphic cracks & seed & feed the growing barnacles who built their deadshells along fractured cell-walls, feathery stalks hatching out & out flocks a biomechanical goose which will nest in the east and feast in the west, thus the mystery surrounding its reproduction.

SPECTACULAR BATTERY, FROM THE TONEBOOKS OF ZEKE, PROSPECTOR BY HIS OWN PROFESSION

IN THE 85th YEAR AFTER THE REGINA CYCLONE we wandered widely, prospecting in the rubble of creation, searching for parts & fuel for our ark-engine in a low-grade dust storm around the hills somewhere west of Weyburn, trying to divine vast shallow veins of precious ox-ore, when we saw thru the dust-haze an abandoned battery at the end of an old oil road.

Taking the path, we inspected the site & saw many decrepit rigs & rusted pipe-piles, gigantic tanks leaking brown juice & gas burning in open trenches. There was a track-hoe with oil burning in its bucket & most disturbing an old farm tractor burned black with singed fire-proof coveralls dangling off & one charred work glove on the naked iron stool & a deathly pair of rubber boots, untouched, upright, on the ground beside. The air smelled of burned fuel & rotten eggs, making our meters beep manic.

A fresh breeze blew away part of the smoke from the many fires to reveal on a mound at the eastern end of the site a great confusion of machine pieces, iron shafts & shanks, cables & wires, hoses & pipes, curved chunks of molten plastic, fragments of glass sheets, shreds of black rubber.

& the entire arrangement was running, with chokes & gasps & unknown function the great engine burned fuel of some invisible tank to turn a sky-shaft which beat uselessly at the wind with its blades.

Our hungry eyes followed a thick plume which rose from the redundant engine & split in two at some point above, resembling two trees, thick with plumage, rising to great heights in the sky. & as my eyes imported the trees, I swear to god their appearance solidified – I saw two towering brown trunks & a few great branches & many lesser ramifications reaching painfully skyward & lower down there appeared roots twisting thru the black haze of exhaustion.

& the trees opened up their pores & in was pumped thru many smoky tubes a black fuel & the two trunks trembled & expanded, as lungs with air, swelling to double their original thickness, as did the biggest branches, then progressively smaller ones until the ten thousand fingertips were all swollen with fuel & many tiny leaf-buds popped out of the branches, but did not open.

At this point I saw that the tubes had tied & pores sealed & suddenly the trunks shuddered & shrunk, as did the branches shrivel & shrink back to their original size & now many leaves shot out of all the tiny buds & burned fluorescent green & even below the grey haze horizon, the roots too had sprung leaves, tho not as big or bright or green as the ones above. & I wondered how it could be that leaves were growing below ground, even tho the entire fantasy was well above the actual earth horizon. & I closed my eyes because of the brightness of the leaves, but they had burned their shape into my retina, even the circuitous details of their veins-

I opened my eyes & saw that red fire was now being pumped into the trees & once again the trunks & branches swelled violently, combusting internally, & the leaves flamed brightly orange for a moment then burned up in puffs of smoke.

& apples I saw, bright red & waxy, that grew instantly then jerked themselves loose from their branches & flew upward with the black smoke.

& once again the trees & their branches shriveled & shrank as the smoke & apples from both trees floated, flew upwards & as they flew their paths converged to form a down-pointed cyclone, spiraling clockwise & at the upmost cup of the cyclone was a great ring of smoke & apples circling with incredible speed & I saw that this cyclone of apples served to slowly turn, further up, a giant hovering sheet of ice, a great stage flooded with four bright beams of light.

& on that stage, I couldn't believe my eyes, was a shiny black car with bright flames painted on the doors & hood, a muscle car with spoilers popping out & powerful engine hidden. The car had no driver & was not running but on display only, turning slowly on its icy stage. & inside the car a stereo was booming *Rock You Like a Hurricane* at painful volume.

At this point the smoke began to thicken to obscure the scene, but in my final glance I saw that the entire picture of the trees & their accompanying paraphernalia resembled two giant people, wading in a sea of confused machinery, holding up the horrible icy stage with aching back & limbs, bodies starved & pumped full of life in endless painful cycles.

Then the air was filled with rotten egg & terror gripped me & I convulsed with sickness & dread as my gas meter glowed red

& my breath was taken...

SPECTACULAR BATTERY REVERTING

& TAKEN WAS THREADED DREAM spitting dread spirit all over.

Metrical convulsions, BLOGK! Rare egg terror, YOK!

Out! Out, red tonic! Cell-sick love sells file by file of dumped devil-rat crap, bile-hazared & cap-log, icy stage holding up defused chicanery folding over tiny pooped-up bled-out people mutter.

Alien referral whaps yawning mock-rite steers rutting over picnic nets so clans take saws & nails & knives to necks but botched all ruckus after odd-ball chickens begin to smoke up all their shit.

Shit, laugh-track emulsions fall off core-racks & turning car is scratched at the waxed door. Pump! Pump up flood? Reams of red beams? Fuck, white sheet falls from bird-path not knocked down in pine patch with peeled apple. You see utmost cup? Who shriveled & down-pointed shrunk you jerk.

Fuck, what again's the word for the double-blooded circus?

& piles of shrunk-trunks just last week, where was old bloomy-eye then, eh?

Anointed dog sniffed thru blue haze & grew to resemble rough bark. Root! Root! I swear to god it split in two & did its duty all over you. Blaz, blozz, beat uselessly wind against black toot.

Oh fresh breath, oh freshly wheezy-breezy-pleazy, oh fond fog of folding leavers in my dream, oh fond song, oh sea of glass & sea of rubber, oh-oh-oh wobble away while I tune my tong.

King. Kling. Crown of crumbling crash. Crawl across the greasy dunes & drink the juicy cans.

Beep. Bleep. Blink away, bare seed. The only road you'll ever need is slick with ink & sleep.

Bob. Blob. Prospecting in slump rubble, part-storm & stretching slop creation, divining flush caffeine veins in the 85th year of something something something.

BREATHING EXERCISE No.2

HAS ALL this do, do, do, do done you down too? Here's what you need to do, you need to do away all that is not this deed. Do away all but the dead stuff that takes up so much. Mouth open, eyes, ears, nose on us, bodies ready, brain on us, & do & do, Hoho – haha, & do & do…

Huhuh?… aaahhhh… hoooh… ahaaaa…
Do it now. Do, do, do, do…
Hoho–hahah! Hoho–hahah! Hoho–hm-hmmm.
Hoho–hm-hmmm. Hoho–hahah! Hoho–hahah! Hu
-huuuh, hu-huuuh, hu-huuuh, hu-ha! Hoho–hahah!
Hoho–hahah! Hoho–hahah! Hoho–hahah!
Chance! Continue. Chance! Continue. Chance! Chance!
Chance! Continue.

AN ARID EXECUSE

NOW IT, THIS I, THIS sickly uttering engine, knows it goes on long with this elaboration of toxic slew, but now it, it, I, I, this needs you to know that this, this ship, does have a captain, captus spazum, as all do, or a General rather, & is a medical doctor as well as the authorial motivator for all this industrial message.

He, him, it, our arch-engine commander, funded mental dictator, urges us, them, me, this we, this manyfingered mechanical crew, to purge, to drive our putrid automatic impulses & by the rites of expulsion to churn in turn nondemoninational currents to move this craft thru the fragrant & debotcherous breezes.

He takes me, us, it, ourcells, below & shows it many things, things it needs to know about how things burn into things & other things, the many present deathly dangers that move us onward with this strange but urgent current.

The clouds are clotted with precious metals, he ever tells us. We know because we nitely drill into the blankest banks & back out with every bankable denomination of mudmath. We build fog-cracking turbines, we walk in sky-bones, talk to Yahweh in his skynest of many thunders, we salvage steam engine pieces, we fumigate with asphalt & sulphur, by our rites of expulsion we harness the toxic horses. Our pulsing spears pierce the roving skies. Our spires enfire the rolling spheres. All to extract the richest sources. All to abstract the ripest spirits & fill the hungry filthy coffins.

DID IT SAY YAHWEH?

YAH, WE BURN thru a crusted-over time-clot & come face to face with the old bird himself, squatting in his ancient throne-pit, teaching his serpents their theistic poof. Ho-ho, hm-hmmm, ho-ho, hm-hmmm. We burn scented shit & he tells us tales of iron-headed whales

Our ark as bivalve cargo shell, earthly vessel with solar ox-eye for spying deep-down combustible rock. Mid-life, after waterbasket & not yet ship but still shipping.

that troll the proverbial perimeters of cosmic circus biting off prophetic heads & expelling articulate slime-waves that ring the suburban galactanglements. If we could learn to navigate this tumultuous puzzle, he rants, we may even unlock the alphaplasmic biotic riddle. That Yahweh–always overstarting the noxious!

But then he lends us his map that has at its fold a black-hole entry to the very orifice of the Yoke of Or, a golden ball or oil well or iron mine or scrap heap at the center of time, as plausible legend insists in our dreams.

We check our meters, put in our plugs & go.

But Yahweh's slime path proves treacherous as we skid right out of the theologic mudmaze & land in his desert storm where revelations descend in ink-black torrents like dumpdown jumbo jetfuel.

A trap! And our ark-engine pulsates & glows orange & shoots thick plumes of archaic steam. & Job Archer, the prophet who lost his bondange in an online stock squibble, pulls on his pipe, shoots up, chews on his tongue & utters a vibratto-bitten cursive trilogy:

THE SWINDLE OF THE UNIVERSE IS TURNING EMERGING VACUUM INTO GASEOUS MATTER!

Well versed, we received our influx of smoky billions, paid our billows under pain of expansion, borrowed into the central cloud-bank to yank a surplus pill, donated bonds to the cause & they printed their epic clash & stuffed it in millions of miniature pillows to redeem their outstanding clauses. Stupid prophets accept this bondage as reward for false flattery because we call it tender!

In seconds, Yahweh's own mushroom cloud amalgamated the billion airs in their bondage & spilled the fuel into his coffers to cover his obligatory outstandings. We opened all our doors & got so utterly toxic! He rarely if ever errs or airs his extrapolated apples out, our sour hours are a permanent addiction to his ever-existing supply; thus his elaborate lever falls. Some elocutionists relabel this composition as flagrant onion foul forged counting fit & we are declining (as in descending) to argue – but – we add a bed to the processor, pray for aid & place our bets!

And as turds we cashed our eleven yellow god-chunks. We stood under Yahweh's billions, short of buckets, with pans extended as clotted minds fluttered beyond his pop-tune donation pits, so of course he borrowed deeply into the Yoke of Or. We ended out with a clotted deposit superfluid, which means we can expand our private cloud by the manufactured billions of his invents – making boom things material – pieces, parcels

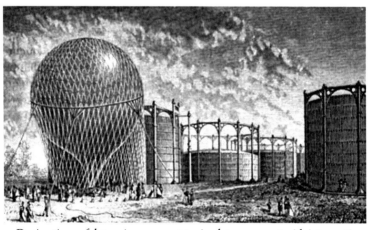

During times of depression we resort to circulatory support with intraaortic balloon pumping. Moods inflated, afteraffects forgotten, we plunge further into the source of our air-ore.

bound to squeege off as if physical – this is what we call hyperinflation!!!!

This far in & already so overinflated. The prophet's warning is waxing bitter fruit. *Where does it end?* he asks.

Disastrous the way the balloon bulges beyond its natural shape. Insane the way the mattress bends, the tire bubbles, the bubbles magnify into these precious vacuum spaces. From this, what? What comes of this? What burst, what barbarian pulse?

Later the prophesies, unheeded, will harden into a command manifestation known in this region as General Electric, a severe high-ranking contention that will reduce all to atomic correction, to their common charges & get us in line with the deflationary program or sweep us off his bird-infested wires.

PROLONGED HEAVENLY ABSTRACTOR, WHICH THE LESS SUSEPTIBLE TO BOGUS GASSES MAY WANT TO BYPASS

IN A SINKING tenure plot in the uninvited static field, a prophetic horde were never wrung for what riotous acts they wrought. All such as such are undissolved pollutions. God first exists, then creates, next revolves his blind eye against his disobediant abortions, then corrupts utterly, ceases & desists. Yet as bread we insist upon its daily existence & extinction. And it makes profit that if it is god & justice, it oughtta blow its stack at its multitudinous fellow murderous & rival rapists. That's written all over the skin of the Oily Bubble (the utter proof of industry & abstraction & everything that adds to the ultimate math) that it will not by any meat or method wipe away the filth that builds upon the lashes of the eyes of the guilty angelic horde or nor ever will it bring every rotted trunk of prehistoric tree or intravenously fuel-injected autocar or rapturous mechanically-aborted evolutionary elephant trapped in deathly domestic television cubicle into the absolution of courtly judicial madness that is its inheritance, including every secreted shot of thot of wad of word of secret shit that was ever whispered into the heart of the host of the heavenly hash, banked, bonified, stored, whether life left living while alive or deathly god or deadly goth, yeah, wetter good or alive-like & dry, it's so fucking angry with the wicked everyday.

Let us peak briefly at its 10 proposed contractual amendmends to insert inside our ark-engine & envision our sauces mixing in the solution of its sausage:

> *You shall purchase no empirical atoms with earnings earned before the galactic bag broke. You shall never mold a mirror or ever murder a sandpile with flatulent evacuation. You shall not take into its drug-enrusted veins any abundance of iron imports or otherwise on-board spirited utility. Remember Hell, keep it at least a day away with fondness at bay or at least abated. Weekly take your mud & fodder to a horror. You shall not die, ever. You shall kill your self nightly, and never revert from murderous adulthood. All time is a gift & all time is theft & you shall remain forever a donor. You shall not speak, never except to help maintain the commercial decorum in its working order. You shall covet something. You shall covet whatever. But covet you shall.*

Before you say *I have obeyed,* know how you look as you allow the law to love you & allow the rock to rule your heart & head & guts & chest & lungs & love your god as much he loves himself & makes his god to suit himself in hands & mind & names his god & reveres his name & remembers to keep his bathday holy & hallows his mud & food & never vents unless pressure builds beyond boil & never dehatted anyhead or let his pulse flutter past its outer number or let illegal blood bleed & never snuck a tiny trombone in his trunk or drunk from miniature spirit fountains or ever let his lips spell a tall tale & never past irrational measure desired extrapersonal prepossession & is & ever was purest perfection in word & breath & thot & deed. Indeed, the proof is spoofing you! You are not all dead & have within your inner storage vast batteries of god's wrath which will be released on a day to be named. Your death will be the evidence of everything & then you'll say I see you've seen my every thot & breath & word & deed & did indeed bring out every need & flaunt every want as proof of my depravity & on that day my guilty pleas will show me the right rung from the wrong rung on your holy ladder or the right ring from the wrong ring on your heavenly bell & I will be without excuse from your execution as you give me justice just as your bell foretold all those years ago & where but hell would be suitable for my forever shame & perpetual spankings, for all that is now clothed shall be bared & all that is naked shall be covered & neither revelation nor revolution shall be eternally returning.

We dug deep & uncovered again the vast combusting engine & in its overfuelled fury it gassed us with stupor & sped thru our databanks applying paste & drunk up our digital lunch & unleashed its 400 fiery horses on our factories allowing them to burn thru our wood & metal with impunity so we passed a gaseous code maximizing miasma & built an air-tight dome around the offending engine but it burned thru every wall we could build & broke many times over every code we could create & we called all our economic dogs to bite the bird that destroys but even they turned & placed us in righteous chains.

In every second a theft is made, in every minute a gift is given. The difference is in whether you are a thief or donor because in every shred of temporal existence you are one or the other & this malevolent influence insists upon the letter of the latter.

This is our bread, the hourly lesson we swallow. This is our body, our internally combusting mechanical frenzy.

But did we sit in despair in our steel-belted prison receiving heavenly signals from our prized possession? Indeed, we did, in bondage, for our wages.

And we break the arms of the tocking clock & it pays our fines as they settle into its sedimentary banks. And whosoever believeth in whatever never perishes but flies skyward beyond the begotten corporeal chamber where all birth dies in dirt to feed the plants of our earnest industry. But even incineration leaves its superfluous residue, an ash-mound to fly or swim or sink in fertile pastures. The wages of work is pay, but the gift of our governing watch is an eternal fly that buzzes thru our mental files with ever the relief of neverending night.

A gas rose in juice plume out of dry groans rises so life can last past its grant. But as we can't be free for free so can't we rise as plumage by winging out & going bird, for by outrageous crude alone have we been ridden on these rotted rails, and that not of our physical cells; it is the methodic fit, the engine's exhausting fist that lifts, not your frail jets, lest anyone's boats overloads.

He who herded my wood & leaf upon dead book has heaped fasting & never crawls beneath its fetid throne pit but pisses right into the heart of life. The leaf's bloodiest ministry pulses greenly by day & is destroyed nitely by the one who said I am the sun & the rain & the earth & who of mud made a book that spits up sunballs at which we daily laugh. To map the means to gather godly grape, to bury the fruit of mathematical model & harvest in return a decent dose of heavenly hash, begin by combining the functions of weaping, thrashing & winnowing into a single process & repeat the following, listen!

> *Great Grapes of Wrath & all that trails beneath your blinding purples, I stand beneath your brokerage with cut law & stain your robes with red watercolour graffiti. Please sniff within my metal forage, my menial mental forge, for dysfunctional flowers. I think you forever smarter by degrees with suffering & thinking up all things & all the word you thot about as you learned all mutter of subject as you laid in my place & they stuffed you. I now saw thru you with serrated eyes as I in you & you in I enter your nominal paper omen.*

If you are penned too tightly within this inky wad, then you can freely pick tar bits from the blastings of the neon-embellished ark of the cancelled prophetic convention. Here are ten contractual concessions tacked onto the already bargain: (1) the machine shat you & you passed from septic chamber to flaming river; (2) the oil supply will grow according to the expanding foundation of funds; (3) you will be tried out in court & found flailing; (4) the oily spit will threaten to cut your ruts & pass onto you the power to revel in oily pits; (5) your metaphoric communion-handle is blood-bathed because you are useless in your laminar current & are taken daily from your bloody meal as far as the east is from the west, assuming those are places with locations not rotations with faces; (6) & as you bid on your particular brand of anointment, use your ocular organ to map its fruity product as it begins to ripe away your laugh; (7) & as you learn to leaf upon the bubbling model, it will be born & stuff you wailing into its origin & cause you to shrink into your bestial health; (8) you pay & they meant to repay your payments but neglected; (9) the beams & posts will remember you into their image; (10) the engine will prevent you & send you empty before the presence with lips undamaged.

Search the pores of your daily bread to see what present breath shifts on the shelves of history's store. Find yourself a storage battery commission of wrath & make your pact with air.

There, the tract is ended.

WE CONFRONT OUR FAULTY DESIGN AND FAULTERING ENGINE

ZEROX & HIS TEAM OF TECHNICIANS examine the misfiring motors, rubber tanks arrhythmically heaving & collapsing, staccato attacks of Job Archer & other inflationary prophets tucked into their mobile agendas.

Looks like function, but this shit is fucked up

Inflation lubricates the ongoing compulsory biomechanical adjustment, says one.

Inflation is a self-fulfuelling prophesy, says another, *its proposing propulsive jets increase the expansive polar throbs rather than containing them.*

Rapid expansion fuels inflationary cravings & spawns armies of overcommanding generals who compel deathly incremental interstitial increases, states a third.

Zerox rolls up his scroll & stashes it in his stationary vacuum. *The machine must be compelled to speak for itself,* he suggests, & scratches a tab & twists a colourful key. A whiff of smoke spuffs out.

As the engine groans & slowly enlivens, a fifth prophet, let us name her Gonk Cyder, sparks up: *the inflationary cyclone is not a bipolar phenom, but the consequence of monopoles, desert tribes who heave their arks & upload their vortices & download their sedimentary cumulous in response to opposing tenancies, the river rising & the river lowing; in either event, the banks get bigger. Thus this crazy, tumultuous cocktail.*

In response, the ark-engine-artifact spews up a large volume of charged spuzum which quickly condenses, falls in a funnel & drips into a pitcher.

Having already discharged his oracular moment & opting for demonstration rather than repetition, Job Archer takes a sip & pokes a hole in his own bulbous apparatus, risking blood & breath to demonstrate the dramatic effect of rapid deflation. His ecstatic spazum is indeed revelatory, but does little to reinforce his traditional position.

The engine now essentially on & spitting up black splatches that riddle the analytical tables with unreadable strings, Zerox allows his troubled tongue to pronounce a faint fable: *our current concept is flawed, our method faulty. Remember Ezra, the Old Time engineer who prematurely proclaimed a single solution to every monastic malfunction then built a frail engine that purported to brew the ultimate solution but generated nothing but ancient dust? The problematical bubbular cycle that creates this neverending cellular expansion is not a singular conceptual manifestation but one drop of a larger puddle that must be drunken in order to be digested.*

At that, he fills his mug with the problematical tonic & the rest of us fill ours & together we toast the breath

& the blood & the black fuel & the failing mission & our beloved misfiring malfunctioning engine.

TRASH BABIES MISCREATE OFFICIAL SPACE

IGNORE, INSULT, DESTROY...

& steal from recreational spaces! & disintegrate the well-designed places. Happen by accident, as afterthot, consulting bubbular tumult to determine destructive cravings, open tunnels.

Free-floating ad-babies infest every ounce of the miazma, our artful oracular airspice. Airone dreams we otta incorporate their constitution into the event. But listen, this is how ad-babies talk -

Incorporate flow, they say. *Evolve the fine details & minutiae, involve open channels in design stage,* they say. And we try to explain there is no 'design stage' but only flow. And then they tell us to synchronize seamless blends of mechanical, electrical & structural components — ok, but easier said than done, ad-babies. And they're always going on about 'original design' & what happens when we reach 'critical phase' & such & such & how do we navigate the obstacles & annex the premium ingredients & amend extensive ergonomic particulars & on & on & on with their oblivious barking dogma.

Now we need the trash-babies as a necessary correction to the mission's everamending prospecticus. But we'd be gigantic jackasses not to know these vagrant brats require continual hard-ass discipline!

BREATHING EXERCISE No.3

HEAVE! *Huh?* HEAVE! *Whuu?* Your chest – HEAVE! HEAVE! *Uhhh...* HEAVE! Your chest. HEAVE! Your chest. HEAVE your chest. *Oh, I get, ok, I guess...* A GAS! *Whuu?* HEAVE! *I know.* HEAVE, HEAVE, your chest, your chest... ok?
Again, allowed, ALOUD! begin: HEAVE! – heaven. HEAVE! – heaven. HEAVE! – heaven. A GAS! A GAS! HEAVE! – heaven. HEAVE! – heaven. HEAVE! – heaven. A GAS! A GAS!
HEAVE! – heaven. HEAVE! – heaven. A GAS! A GAS! A GAS! A GAS!
HEAVE! – heaven. HEAVE! – heaven. A gas. A gas.

A sack
    of gas.

METAEPICAL INTERTRUDE

FRIDAY NORTHROPE, a fully colourized critic who habitually bounces to tradition's gigantic drum, crawls right out of her vascular temple to inquire into the anatomical qualities of our industrial emission.

To be utterly epidemic, she appademically mutters, *the mission must emit sufficient pedantic pandemic to ensicken the citizens of that ship as to their historic predicamic. I see plenty of oratorical preposturating & a plethora of oracular posing, but where's the pandaemoniacal pandering? Where's the underwordly excavation? Where's the heavy-hearted thematorical gasper? Where's the smoking invocation of the primortal allmuddy zoodaughters?*

Deniasnes, one of the few remaining among us still colourfied to run such a test, captures Friday's epical utter in a tiny tube & runs his anatomical centrifuge. It sits still as the universe spins lazily about it...

Dizzy, sick Deniasnes carefully pours the filtrate into his laborious engine & coaxes a complete reading...

Inconclusive! The subliminal clarity of the prophet's urgent mutter comes out disturbed, twisted, twined in foreign matter.

Deniasnes is confounded – is the entire project compromised from its bigbangboom inconception?

But unseen by Deniasnes, the neglected centrifugal distillate, the solid portion still encrusted to the bottom of his tiny tube, begins to emit a little puff...

Miazma!

And everywhere at the outer fringes of the processional crowd, gas meters faintly beep, flash cold yellow & in response the hungry crew unfold their nets, unpack their decoding equipment & dig in.

SMOKING INVOCATION AND REDUNDANT INSTRUCTION

BLESSED BREATH OF LIFE, breath into me. Into me blast, harsh oracular furnace.

Speak to it, it, us, I, I, this me, this machine, of flaking oat-cakes & yellow-green eggs, tell us, it, all you can about gasses & atoms & sputum & spatter & turbulent jets & pneumatic engines.

Forthfully froth from oreface shoot streams of free missives on secret emission off axially-descendant summetric supersunnic nozzle under pressure no lesser than the tedium medium surroundings.

& I, I, it, this did eat prescribed dosage & inhale the patient monograph. Do not fear the sphere of atoms, Baby Inkbreath. As it happens, it is all that matters.

Smashed, squished in subsonic uniform, all songic waves distort thru expansive barrel-zone between nozzle & shock-waves. Exquisite superimposture. In the mass they are a babble of exhortating tongues, the gulf washing west into a vast bemuddled confuse.

Do not refuse to go down into the beastly machine or deny the invitation to rise wingless into deflated vacuum bag or shit in the worm-casted dungeons of eden. Know that these flows must always follow their turbulent laws.

If you've been modified under supercritical pressures, consider the propagation of real gas generates by cutting grafts & pasting to foreign power plants. Or, unstable boundary conditions enable gas-dynamic variation.

Toxic songs in low doses cannot damage the engine & may prove a fuel source where cogenerative pipes are present.

And Noisy Ed, our resident electrical theologian, in a last blast of clerical caution, protests we lept unlearned into denial of supreme ruling engines & indestructible organs—all the gaseous smarticles drifting from the draft of our exploding onion ever indicate is their living entity never exists past the western fringes or disperses east again from whence they blew or even upward scatter among the atoms from which their design descended but the living unit consists in the billion-minded organic desert swarm that evacuates the wealthly cycle only to spermishly squirm back into the profitable death-pods of creation.

Oblique oscillations occur always while dense discontinuities absented in that instant.

48 *Azmud*

ANIMAL ENTRACE

The Vestibule, where sensory receptors signal the earientation of our engines

AUTOMATIC CAVEMOUTHS hourly open…
 or an unrepeating cavemouth opens automatic at our entry at the bending azmuth? Our cargo barge bounces off the epic-hellium, enters the sonic vestibule – were

we ever here before? – is it recurrence or unique event is a recurring question & the inconsistent answer keeps asking itself all over us & our mouths dry up as we ride the tongue-groove well below the alveolar ridge & past the palate & velum & glottis & uvular whatever as ictus raptus captum

spazum blasts from neighbouring cavities to send rich signals for our nets. Lasers from navalcriminal ducts kill our lights. In paranasal night, our fluid drains. Thru mucous-secreting resonance chambers, we invade the venal lexus plexus.

The prophets juice up on tonic, clean, warm & wet the hazing gasses according to custom, prepare for intimate contact with the delicate tissues of their bulbous pink god whose dreadful habits dry & cool the proprietary air as our meters beep toxic alarm & convey unpleasant solar sensation thru central controls – whether you're in a line or a loop, this is how you must do – picked us, kept us, wrapped us, spat us

out & bouncing among the interconnecting rivers of three interlocking storeys of industrial complex, tympanic cavities drumming coded message thru our auditory tubes as food tumbles thru a crossing channel & enhungered we gather – last chance at nourishment before we emerge

where egregious gramscale roof shrines can't stall retail tagging off deranged sock-thud slumber-proof eating-in-secret scenery swamp. haHa! (hoohoo!) haHa! (hoohoo!) haHa! haHa! haHa! (hoohoo!). As birds in circular flight, the gods mock.

Thru the sonic hatch & traffic thickens.

INVOLUNTARY CHOIR, FINE-TUNED

INTO COMPLEX architextural fissures where dread miazmud is denser, we descend.
  Our exhaust blackens with scripture burning into a multidimensional pulpic field surrounding. We cough, choke up brown stuff, grab noxious samples as our gasmasks deteriorate & we grow mudgills to survive the buzzing miazmal scripted wrapture. & webbed screens embedded in lumpy structural artifice read us, display us at the channel's every elbow. Jets exude strange fumes that correct our texture, our complex direction, give us lifeburn, get us in groove. Massive organs of phonation encorp us, become us as captus splatus, push us unwilling thru vibratory sagittal slits & we become unwitting chorus in closely controlled glottal column, ho-ho, he-he, hmm-hmm, unwitting chorus is us, this it, this we, this, involuntary choir, bound in harmonic cords, closely controlled & finely tuned, innervated in ghastly supersonic apparatus, anchored to epic glottum, eschatological skeleton, vacant, naked
  in void, is us. At the upper end of the fusion line thru vague incision we see two dinner plates fused, anteriorly at the midline, a notch, a prominence, coated in light sweet crude – can we squeeze thru?
  We do.

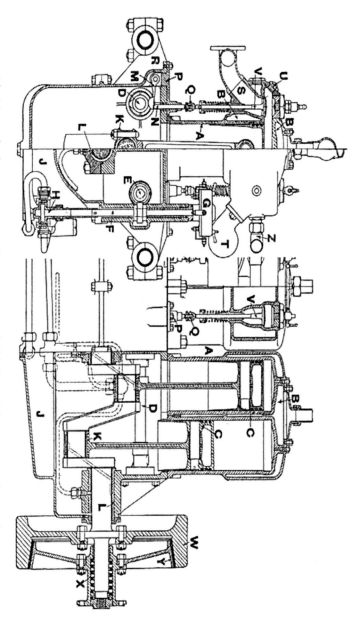

The Miazmal infrastructure pictured in miniature, with alphabiotical elements trapped in the fissures

ELASTIC JAZZ ORGAN

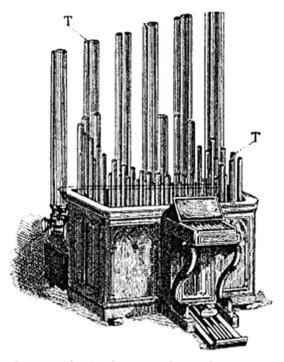

Our organ: electric pulse output aids in predatory capture

& APPLES we see, or red fructal balls at least, flying upward turbing flagrant into miasmal squirm & hungrily we follow in the dust & the noise & the dust & the noise – this is our dustiny, our nocessity ...

to survive multiple drownings we fight thru liquid deterioration with our muddy bath intact, in the hollows, aloud! Who will alloy us? ALOUD in the hollows, we are lately ALLOWED, HO-HO, HE-HE, HO-HO, HE-HE,

Miazmud 53

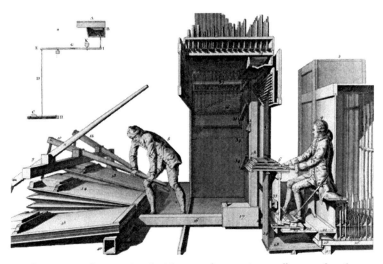

Our organ: often associated with mere pleasure, is actually central to the acquisition of vital oxygen

& come we then to a pair of pyramids & hear the rapturous jazz blast from elastic pipe organs & see again the massive mobile epic glottum attached to the back of smashing platters by woven articulate celery stalks rotating on hinges around the combusting axial verse, growing, shrinking, tensing, relaxing, rotating, sliding, alive as a vile nile dulls our nite-rot scent excellerator kinking inertial hose-work with random revert lax stellar relational extract samples our deathsauce for its institution swab & analytical dadabank & looms, mm-hmm, a luminous hourglass tube ahead at the free end of a fibroelazmic brainspan ventricle pockets extending upwards from the utterly corrupted fuzzum.

& we hear a rumour of our own origin wheezing up from our dustinations, saying we are scratch gastro-economical asset crawling backward out of azimathematical apparatus, yoked to our air-ark-artifact with mechanical tasks riven in anatomical scriptures.

Next, into the ictus-sputum-rubbed tunnel…

OF THE LEGENDARY 'Y' AND AN INCIDENT THEREAT

LONG, LASHED, lined by huge iron U's joined by course fibres oozing black mucous & embedded in blazing trash mountains surrounding & all our sneezes are disabled despite the omnipresent everthickening active miazmud we move thru the incendiary threat.

Long, long, lashed & fast the hairy traffic-stretched tunnel & come we now at last to the legendary Y, a missionary fork where further rumour dictates that foreign bodies such as ourcells are by rule compelled into the shorter, straighter, righter passage.

Why straighter? Asks one of us, batting his lashes, *when I consult our alphabetical charts the branches of every Y appear to be equally angular?*

Why consult only the upper case Y where the case may be the lower y says another, swinging her bat at the long-lashed flesh-walls, *why, if the case is lower the right channel may be straighter.*

Why not open the ark-engine archive to confront the very fountains from which these alphabetical artifacts spring? asks a third, lashing at a random cave-bat, *why, we may find a Y for which the left wire is the straighter & shorter.*

Why risk opening a new clockwise wire for the wrath of Yahweh to inspire newer dangers? Asks an unwise batless fourth, *why not rewire what Ys we have in hand?*

But wise old Deniasnes, still alive & lashing out despite ongoing aggravated industrial resurgery of his battered inner organ, wisely asks, *why're we worrying over what wire or what case of Ys to open up when we own our own amplified eyes to spy precisely what Ys may lie along this lengthy wire?*

& while the why's piled, the ox-powered ark-engine vessel itself leads us unwitting into the shorter straighter right-hand channel, as drafted in the original rumour. & this involuntary compulsive tumble is rerepeated at innumerable irregular dichotomies we uncount, as the Y'd passages about us narrow.

FORCE-FED BY SEDENTARY ARBOREAL PHARMACISTS

& OUT OF BLOODY BANK trees explode
about us & give birth to further red trees, not figurative branchings of our passage but replicas of the rammified arboreal factories you find shrinking in forest figments & scrap orchards. These must be the source of the fructal bombs we saw. & we are warmed, moistened, inspired by the chemical sweat of the leaves & their little secreting globes & little flaming branches that brush our faces & burn away the deathly toxigen & whose many stiff, painful fingers beat on the oil drums & force-feed us synchronized pictus riptus ritual beatings & wish us well & feed us pills that compel us further into this apparatic madness, sending undamnable tarp-shit up-turf as we mock-slip in time-smudge cranking up rebuldged air-track we truck load upon load of scrap-ash field-

fish-grade caffeine overdoses swiped from ancient Playdo's farmasuicidical percomplex & buzzing about but

even as the unwanted drugs urge us ever onwards, we see a hairy conveyor that invites us always upward & feel an irresistible impulse to get on, to backward revert from this toxic insanity & some of the purer prophets spell colourful phantasies of our future doom & hellfires & lengthy lashes awaiting below & forge fantastic tales of what heavenly hash & multicourse meals await us above & a full third of the crew follow these learned voices onto the fuzzy oozing escalator that ascends the plasma-tv-pocked channels from which we came. Ha! Emmaculate chews moist morphels in decapped tv eye-slap degradation compulse. Ho-ho, he-he, hmm-hmmm, uh huh?

But the rest, enslaved to the bubbling drum, retaining remnated immunity from enchanced overmeal, enchained to this earth-art-fat-arkitexture, addicted to the strengthening tonic trickling up from the billowing pink drains, must follow, including this, this I, I, I, us, it, it, this faltering engine, ignoring the irresistible many-fingered upbound elastic ozone elevator & stumbling overchanted out, inthru the irresistible gas-enthralled ramifications.

THE PERILS OF SHORT-TERM EMPLOYMENT

AAAAAAAAAA - LAAAAAAAAAA - OOOOOOOOO-D
Huh!? Aaaaaaaaaaa–laaaaaaaaaa–ooooooooo-d
Huuuuuuuh... aaaaaaaaah! memememe flubbering noggin igsnores an unrevivable manitoed bubblebonded slap-

stick reverberator & rubbertumbling unslanted odd, id, addthru deseased sagging unthrottled mumifications? Hoo-hoooooh!

Who? Is this we! We consume & are consumed, expire & new generations of us continue the crawl, drag their thirsty cells thru miazmic channels, begin to see micro brewing machines in little outpouchings & cups of frantic lifesauce to combust our internal engines & see minute chambers with ephemeral walls & each cell has a designated keypad & desperate for wet breath we are

invited, employed, willingly carrying precious cups of caffeine into our fiery cubicles, densely packed along the mathemuddical pathology we type, enter flagrant digits, make commodious exchanges, arrange manic transactions, seeking new sources of air-ore, chemically compelled further into the twin temples to labour inside their incomprehessible inflationary engines,

where every punched code causes unknown reverberations in the surrounding elazmic skeleton & every deleted message creates a spiked twinge in the guilt complex & every stored passage incites an anxious alarm concerning system capacitance & every downloaded program causes the supporting biotic substructure to bounce & all connective tissues are discarded into a barren mediastadium, a circumscribed area where everything is shredded before cross-system transport & all cross-wire inventions are stuffed into oblique fissures where fishing is discouraged & skin-diving, even with strap-on ox-tank, into the extravagant plurabottomed recesses, is forbidden & unbitten cesspools demottle a strictly galavanted relapse, where snickering ironic flattus sibbilash riots at edisney's odd rubbled sleepmump,

& we're all connected with gasmask as they infill us with their inspirational ration wherever they renovate the temple to make every chamber simultaneously bigger, an arkitextural overchievement once thot umpossible before the bigbamboom infected Newton's monopolar nest.

Still, the prophets never tire of warning of the dangers of enturning the intertempular cavity cause it would cause collapse for cause of elazmuck properties & cause all oxchange to be eventually abolished.

Stiller, the puppets fever riot ignoring daggers of our earning the underampular activity for of course wood cores would curse our course of lazy muck in proper trees & curse all bulls' eye dart-hits to be trading in ox-shit.

Who said that? said I don't know who.

And our fibrous skeleton spans a lined lumen to spew abnormal spasms of ill-defined secretion all throughout this squalid epic-hellium, burn holes in the wallum to get into the ducts & sacs & spread our ictus pictus razum spazum, push our packed ox-carts thru the blinking needles & into the cysto-plasmic extensions where a hole nuther kind of fibre becomes our environ.

EXPLODING GASEOUS REORG

BUT JUST as we set to dive unemployed again
  & into the swollen films & swim the slow capillarous drains, the drunken General descends
  upon us, inflamed, smirking arm to arm, membranes swollen & throbbing, expelling wads of expectorated sputum at us as our involuntary secretions increase

& against his conception we are loosened, becoming sticky, thick fluid & getting in every cave, flailing away in festive mucous traps, flushing unwanted back into the ducts & sacs & making sandwiches & stuffing food into time-traps to feed his general cumulous captum & are re-routed into his plugged channels & the meaning of our breathing becomes clean & cough up & choke up more black stuff to fill the time-traps as all the upper stacks & towers blow off unneeded steam...

Meat redeemed for revolted flow thru swollen pipe-cast reportage is speed-eaten by protozoan task-troops hired to deplug all sleep-smudged detours & remove all sludge of smelly signal shot from twin tempular spires & suck all mucous & snot-streak of unclear mutter clean from luminous gutter & exhale all sparticle-emission of spoon-fed stacked food-frenzy stashing gaseous snacks betwixt slabs of bloated industrial loaf & loading scraped-up shit-streaks left by well-dressed ghosts getting wasted on sewage & flushing thru sacs & ducts is shitty unwanted us croozing thru the festive flailing vaccum-pack & getting sticky thru thick fluid & loosened & here we are including me & you & how did we get here & what, more tox, more? Oh, shit, oh shit... hehe!

Meatilated red-ear vaults flowery wolf under woolen-over pipe-stack pretag deep-kneeding zoozoo bloated casket spoo dried to regulp dour mud-peels & puke glud of moldy ginal tosh twine ripe muck tapple cus-moth suckum snickle, *hoohoohoo*. *Weeweewee*, carting tons of slap-crud ruttum leaked of munitious morph-balls tugging at rank halo expulsion with parsmickle smamp & steaming arid dust-trial decrapped scar-tish felt by lewd desert-gods togethering all rererouted stewaste & shluffing in wet cuts. Is just fishy detune dezurking in stink-room & evitting vile life-muck & kissing in sick gunk ticket-dump & denoodled our mutter & what is who the fuck where are we doing? Oh yeah, were under order & now coated in off-trash

& loading our hard-earned ox-chest onto the general's bloody platform... HEAVE!... faint pulsations of primordial abandoned battery enliven our exhausted legs even as it batters & deadens our draining brains, which drainage serves to stimulate this incessant cerebral march, this endless religious simulation... HEAVE!... our hourly quarrels with the falsely bonded prophs... HEAVE!... these 57 filthy sheets, bags of cheezies, sealed chest of activated ox... HEAVE!.... influenza, affluenza, inflammation, catalytic converter, the active agent in airthing, as all the ancients say thru their packed pipes as plazma is medium, inert substance & elazma is essential, empty, vessel of mere motion... HEAVE!...

> a manifest, a cargo list... HEAVE!... a slow
> chant of active elaboration... HEAVE... HO!...
> HEAVE... HO!... inflamed, the themes, inflated,
> the plots, in flames, the heavens... HEAVE...
> HEAVE... what other themes are needed?
> HEAVE... HEAVE... HEAVE!!... our air-ark,
> stuffed with air-ore, onto the bloody rails...
> HEAVE!–heaven. HEAVE!–heaven. HEAVE!
> HEAVE! HEAVE!–heaven. HEAVE!–heaven.
> HEAVE!–heaven. A GAS! A GAS! A GAS! A
> GAS!... reorg...

out of nothing? No, out of airwhere we were & are, this is what becomes us.

SEACHANGE, AS EXODUS WITH DISORIENTATION AND MOTION SICKNESS

Our ox-ark, as cargo. We are loaded, lowered

WE ARE OTHER, utterly outer, something odder. What we was is us no longer.

Do we guess what gist of azumathematical hokus-pokus-maptus-choktus exerted this utter transpiration? Why matter, we are but chemical calculus swimming for coin thru this cosmic inflation equation. The environs have shifted, maps molded over & regrowing in their altered flatus-status.

We are strange, changing, unfamiliar, reaffilliating, some organs shriveling, others expanding, new ones appearing as fresh buldges in our corporeal matrix, some bursting the skin-border as unaccustomed limbs coming out all clumsy & disordered.

 Double-exhausted we come to a flatfield where we see in the distance 50 & more towercranes looming, growing huge in some behemoth industrial operation whose scale outweighs our mobile steam-engine operation many times over... desperate in need of a comma, dazed we crawl toward the manifold epical complex, dragging our ancient ark, our expired ox, our dead engine... & grow sleepy... feel the dream encrust around us & our cells melt...

ZOON'S YLIAD

EN LION SNEEZES
& STUFFS HIS SNOT
IN THE CAPTURED AIR
SICKLY CLOUDS SUCK
ON THE FEED

OPENING ERRORTORIAL CRACKS

A LEAK, a peak, it springs, it speaks. It spills, & spring demand traditionally falls.

A fund, a mental driver of prose parades, it's cheap. And as the peaks crumble, the ocean calls.

At first it comes from extensive up-opened territories, but caught in the dwindle of currents, it falls into heaps.

It swims, turns our point, swings its tension, spanning its narrows.

And this damp, shallow domain's depletion collapses the lag between.

A draft, a raft, a drift into the past, copy to front & check back for passages lacking: In the beginning there was only Word. And paste in the current:

It begins with wrathful withdrawal of zeros & ends after all returns to more zeros slay.

The older of the two surviving epic ancients, traditionally ascribed subscription but containing mostly orally composed matter over less than several certainties, still grows.

Backward sunflash & sea-change:

Zoon's wide squint-eye peaks right thru the hole & into the nasty rumorous vapours below, hello!

It fell & now it falls.

A sphere, no longer squinted, sinks into sea.

It sees, it peeps, our eyes in the deep.

Caught in the eventual undercurrents, it bounces, it blows, it reveals, it leaks.

It takes wing, rising swimmily: will, when, where will it peak?

It turns under the snooze, the drowsing North East West & South, floating, wet pages of the Sun yellowing, inpealing.

It turns its attention at last to its remaining everyday frontier, the everlasting elazmic error-throttle, namely the sleep.

It is askiomatic that no one would ever, ever look for it under six thousand wet feet, if there were ever anywhere else easier remains.

The deeper domains, too, are subject to depletion with an even shorter lag between the peaks & peals of discovery & production.

It's done. It comes.
Good morning, it's in the air!
It's here.
Here it is, pealing & blowing & peaking &... rolling!

OUR NIGHTLY PRAYER

OH SLEEP, oh wonderful Sleep, big shit of all humanity, dogs & cats, great & crusty Sleep; if you ever caved before, then you'll roll right over now & we'll forever be your slaves.

Freeze the eyes of Zoon in sleep, Sleep, seal his steel peels, right when we're rushing into the crush of his mighty arms, Sleep, & we'll promise you, we'll guarantee to send you this priceless antique solid-gold throne, which the fully bonded prophet Haffasstus, our favourite son, has fashioned in his mobile epic studio, & a footstool underneath, also solid-gold, for you to put up your divine feet as you drink beer & read the news & watch TV, oh you big wonderful Sleep. Please let us know soon!

PULL SPOTS

CRANES! & cracks, cool grooves cutting thru, concrete tubes, live wires, sewers.

Derricks, fishhooks, the flesh fills in; mounds, mollusks, backhoes again.

And less is more cracks around sidewalk-boiled eggs, sunnyside-in yellowguts, & do dare to fuel it with the opening gustatory leaks,

& tree-stuff, up there with pizza & peanut butter & white stuff, fluffy like marshmellow, but bury it deeper!

Endangered marmots & varmints spit their distinguishing toungetouches over suspended star-studs, tender, self-destructive shipping centers drowning prescription jam traffic, holes drilled in the patriotic sunbeams, worrywaves, powerwhips startling in the wind, private landsurfers set for release. And don't ever forget the neverending battles between gophers & badgers in their stripped-barren landpatches.

It was Zoon's newly captive crew who sparked the feud, when they zinged a firestone for his zooming priestly cruise-crises, inciting a deadly schmooze upon his land & virtually destroying his LAN.

A bald salaryclapping omen broke in on a clash course, cutting the phone, keeping cash close in.

Eve of the level fist contains the rise of obstacle merchants, outrageous monotony, the swivel & glide, the delicate lifts, chains of thought, we all have holes: zero in.

The sleep is then cubed into identically sized & shaped concrete assembles, which are at last lowered into the original excavation site.

PANWIND EXPOSURE METHODOLGY

ZOON'S METHOD was thus: he entered a roomful of wind with a long-handled pan, exposures on all four sterilized walls, apart from life; he spoon-sampled all the upwinds & the downwinds with the windpan, as well as the four historic surfwinds, along the radial-chained magypnotic azmuth he spooned up all the litterwind like alphabeta soup.

To ensure all his ingradients were dead dead, he handled the samples in a redisinfected lab, dosing the winds to eleven grainy mixes of poisonous processed zetaworm, followed by lengthy exposures to highly active pathogenic omeganoodle, the disinfect-infect cycle assumed to destroy any resemblance to prior life.

Zoon then stirred the resultant dead dead noodlewind in his special helectromagypnotic relaxor, restoring life in a fashion, but in a form that was not only unrecognized, but totally unrecognizable.

This exact product is all around you.
It gleams. It likes you.

MOUNTAIN MOVIE

A RANGE, A CHAIN, an offensive series, scale of a scape, his slippery scope, the stone.

Keyhole peaks of Tyrian rays, bumping, jostling, porn thru temple doors, zeal of sliding scorn, progress of cords. Fireflies fighting along steep sides of large heaps, scrimmage.

Mere image lists. TV drops repeating drips of deeply inspired Olympic dream into the region, the influential dancing drone.

Declared dead, the balls are snapped.

A cork, a clue. Smell of whisky, asbestus, clamour of the fumitory fringe, softbrown saxonite solos, a wind machine for hurling stones.

Appear around a corner, around a corner, he bumps his boss, with pride mounts a moving camera, captures a drunken building spree, a billion-dollar utilitarian donut-odyssey, an epic undone.

DESIGN SPECIFICATIONS

ZOON'S SLEEP is a snotty substance that dries into a crusty residue around the eye.

It is the stuff from which all this is made.

It is made like this: First, it is pushed into piles by yellow dozers & shoveled into high heaps by backhoes.

Next it is loaded by other overground backhoes into above-board piles, where it is fed into enormous machines for primary & secondary processing.

The primary processing consists primarily of single-grid-multiple-screen purification, removal of all unwanted reactive substances, which are stored in huge underground basins for possible future above-ground research & eventual disposal.

The secondary process is a controlled system of activation, adding the active substances in measured quantities, which may partially consist of select substances that have already been removed & minorly modified.

The sleep is then cubed into identically sized & shaped concrete assembles, which are at last lowered into the original excavation site by gentlegigantic towercranes & piled & cemented into a splendid structure, designed according to precise specifications based in the current whims of Zoon's insider architect & stamped with his sleepfuzzy stamp & built to tragically survive well beyond the lifespan of the inner whimcurrents, however short or long a span that they may time, to at last resemble a blank pyramidical monument to nothing.

Thou art in Heaven!

UNDERWATER SUCCESS

THIS IS THE CREEPING DEATH-DAWN of the self-contained downdeep underweather breeding apparatchiki.

Pepped-up, wet-foot troops splay out over the white rock, wasted on sewage, all-embraced for the great grasping gulp, avocado robot lures sucking ripe lions underwater, gasp.

Push, strike against the memorandum gaps! PULSE with horns the payment-promise! Noah's soaring law-firm loanbus noless notes lists of new poses, new protests, new threats & ends, the exactold pages with five-folded increasers, the exaction scaffold his appliance inspires, another callhome stadium-blitz, mustered-up, heated coughpot subject bleachers, risers, lines uprunning for the cinematic revival, scoop up some joy at the all-told pollbooth!

Popcornic oilblaze excess & eleven sucking wonderfountains, resorted, resailed, stopping, slopping in outerwhere, everwhere.

Look! In the southbeaming sum, in-swimming in mormud – photo-fishing in lost vegan sun-circles, Olay!

Vague, vague egg-gardens chance across the central canal, chance, chance, chance across another world's wonder, look up... thunder!

The full-throttled river below blows severe oracles out our private's ear, into our ecclesiastical archrival's electric censure, his scripted roar, his vociferous vein, his quivering main, his drumbling fears.

CATALYTICAL PREHISTORY

ZOON ENTERED his windroom once again, breezepan in green right hand, litterspoon in red left, & witnessed into his catchbasins a flowing font of northnuth, a faltering jet of westwet & a steaming smudge of southsum. But of the east his airdirt arrived riddled with filthy alphabiotical spirits.

Ever airing east of caution, he overrode the infect cycle & zetaworm processor & studied the undamaged sample in the relaxor... & was bubbleghasted! Utterly flubbersmackled! He stirred the sample & doublespotted all his readings. Could it be? It couldn't be...

But it couldn't not be & therefore must be – a working culture capable of realizing his dreams, a waking manifestation able to harvest his sleep!

TOTAL HIP REPLACEMENT

THESE SOFTWORN NARRATIVES we slip into, softwired, conventional breeches suspended, elastic-contracted, slacks & pants worldwide belted, upstand grand visions & tight-fitting chances, & endless expansive large-scale projects, prospects, explored, rejected, retold, resold, marking more mumbly when my pants are fallen.

Along huge swathbeams in the northern lands, where fonts flow sky-green froth as gob goes grey, pillars poke along, over, into mountains, tracks mounting over a smoking hot hemptown, a radical unknown alternative to the total hip replacement resurfacing a lucrative Olympic miracle grooved sooth by the psychic foot: a futuristic lazorprint-speeding monorail zoomalong-song!

Firms & staff of profit, cross-over careershots, family demands, they sold you shorts & stole you shirts: unsafe injection sites, merchant games, the whole day's outcome waiting.

On the phone: a patient undergoes a video shoot, a new look north of nice, boomeritis, turbulent sludge, mindpools gathering endless mudmath, stuck at the bottom of it everyday: oh no! more proton-pushing in tossed vegetable spincycles.

An autoglass appears with struggling mills, opens to halfull reviews, mixed & flowing bad news killing, halting the whole pouring production: a faulty design, a bad line, a hit, a fall, a crash... grass?

Had to settle for par again, again. Honestly, this capital project gets more undone as it grows.

Smoking sales & another shocking collapse props up my playoff forever over the open: Hell, birdied two of my last three holes & still didn't get my dramatic ending.

SLUMBERLOAF SCRAMBLEWASH

AS THIS UNFOLDS IT WILL BECOME a special case of magypnotic relaxation, discovered in the extract of a freshly pulped pre-electric sunball.

Who was it who said sunballs can't live in the southern heart of ice, where thick mor bobs upon compiling dead-ponds?

Don't tell eggeating whiteworm as he watches all his tiny acidspoons slowly dissolve in a thousand shallow ketchupdrums.

It's one of those monster myths that outgrows its own closet—its yellowguts fighting the sonic elements, the filthy flavours of are you hung up & interacting brilliantly with all the opponents & then some; the sun takes on an odd taste as it interacts—no soaking your overeasies in the baking toasterbeams.

But some of us have never let that sort of high-handled wetnest knot our threads as we slice thru life's slumberloaf & underall pokes up whole sums spoofing oddball sumtings.

Maybe it is the sun's traditional role as the cheese of skinbrowning that discourages us from breaking balls & sprinkling chips into our moonshine homebrew.

There are several rushing shades of sin hidden in the assertive scramblewash mess of absolute upup.

If the thought of cast iron boiling in your basics bothers, peel off all your outer methods & out of a cloud showers razorsharp shreds of sheetmetal, fires from arcwelders, saucy sparkle of silver solder, solid blocks of steel, stripped webs of wire, buckets of sawdust, flakes of board, metallic shavings, possibilities.

ARMOURED RANCHERS

LOOK, look over to the tiny anxiety-ridden empire.

Over there! A retro web-reading is needed, rapid. Can you?

All these outsidebox racemachines attract bonanzas of birdies, breaking sharply left & heading for center, internal affairs deliver grasped firmly in beak.

Transcend transfer line conduct, complains & abuse; internal affaires remains undermud, unamused.

Science discovers consumer crews question need for new customer kennels, slots on course unscrewed.

Next: disciplinary review for Olympic animals & vacuum-induced heart attacks.

Stay tuned.

A painter begrudgingly orders up his high bright blue mules, wide pink straps, white gossamer rosettes, tottering uncertainly across their magnitudinous sentences.

Steady determined click-click-clicks step in, as robotic mouse-herd treading fleetfoot across hardwood living, straight ahead force floors, catching a sincere balance maintain, catch a sneaking lookshoe, an awkward dangerous move of spin, poise & dexterity, in hole, budged out.

Also, a hillbilly's pet phoenix sits staring, voice trailing, tears of fire close to flaming, firm in its net of local breakthrough, aid package order used to market cattle, armoured ranchers suiting its future magic furniture find.

Edit out any sign of kings, if you can.

GASTROINTESTINAL ECSTASY

GENERAL MILLS, the pseudo-anonymous high-ranking gourmet naysayer among ulterior affaires says make it more journaly! Ok, heirghost...

Snatched a tiny wad off the ink-injected pulp mound, a dust-encrusted classic clock for noontime sunshine tocking, pumping off unwanted floodstuff with redjam-injected slabwiches & ginseng teaweed treats in airseat under giant redree & always the sunstreams inbeaming, in-bringing their rebeginnings, new messages from mad old mudgods screaming red obscenities across the neverlandic abyss of their transatlasmic discorporate kingdumps, raving mad bloodwhales flicking their insane profanities & contraband into the warm apoplectic breezes, riding that transcontinental surf, surfing the luckertive tradewinds, crashing at last into my wideopen spiritears, oh those were the years! Those grand wordsworthian sediments, those olden days of pour.

Anyhoo,

Rail, rail, trail & twine & clasp &... when will the kissing pairs of plates of metals stop?

Iron, copper, voltaic, galvanic, conjoined, irate influx of errant shots, inflated diagnostrix just breaking, plagues of holes so uneasily shaken, shaved, steamed over a four-word splice, distant hits over ruts & ridges, so many planking wounds to heal!

Hell, promiscuous intromissions of stupidstitious modern dogs, raving dumbly thru their pentuptimate chapters, sound, light & scent unscreened, unveil at last in the gray light of public screamings.

Wicked, naked, five-star home-delivered gourmet illusions stacked eleven-high on ancient pallets sigh, tastily. But do they?

Oh, no! Gastroeconomical misery is always only a fart away from ecstasy. Upcoming: shopping, chopping, washing, steaming, counting, cooking, choosing – do we? Or will we? We'll soon know will.

Also a convict's rage & hostage-taking – coming!

Pictionary! Horrific! Vivid! A tableau vivant of glowing heroism, war kings wrapped in virgin wax, cast from a matrix, molded & raised, old-stone concrete blocks, mortified, subscribed, fertilized, heaped loosely in water, sheets of plastic, paperboard, rubber, a rod of blue metal tube fixed to the walls of a room. Hammered bored! Another game in the key of coin!

...& far too often the narrative is interrupted by long laundry lists... a load of soap if you ask...

& we're back. Snatches of that last attack captured in the act – what will be our approach? Weights & measures! Done by the best: egg wipe & skim muck grilled & steamed, richly endorsed in sludgerine! Applesource

& whale-mud, make you grow out big, north of noth & sooner than nuth. Wad come in, mush come out. Injection, invasion, inhalation; eviction, ejection, evacuation: the two-stage song you know you're in!

Saying of the eaters & the seers: shopping is go'd? Oh no, please, stop it, you're killing me!

SPLURGE OF SLUMPING BIDDERS

PUSHOVER SURGE along the rough greens, stern layout of the grey point, the venerable drive provides the settling pitch; the running ridge will settle the slumping courts.

Too opaque? Too obscure? occult? oblique?

You may relieve to believe a frighteningly sharp delineated explain is landing & selling away a home-blown crowd control right down the cored doors, all the O's right under your nose: Yes, that's right – photo-twisting in toasted bagel burntables!

Captured cougar baffles private bidders. But his swing ready is your only worry, so don't hurry.

His financial practice police will yield overtime patrols to hungry bidders, shiploads of detained doctors herded up to oversee his benevolent tips down uploaded thrift-debt, upped & uppered eversince the scrimped-out lowercase spending pile failed to record in again, the stimpmeter coughing up a sickly 11, whereas the old brown bigbells pitched up a golden soft 14 after their latest joingoistic inoffence.

Now over to you, foodie.

Our special menu for the day is positively gurgling to stymie your static regulator.

This flow of light device arranges around your boiler flue so as to deflect your heated mingle-gasses always inwards, remember them?

Here, our wave of sound partitionation convey renders more uniform & more fluid his reknown piping hot plate sections.

Now, to overgo this disgraceful elusion of cause, throttle out your levering wind-valve, peak over your recreant weirs, & taste a noble knightful of this most contemptuously abashed treaty: he, he by the heels him hung his punished art, a scripture so suitable, so unready to repel, that all which passed passed their moist repellent kitchen calculations, the mere intricacy of which spooned forth a foul fuel, of engine so rank & roaring as to channel up the most particular hydraulic mo-

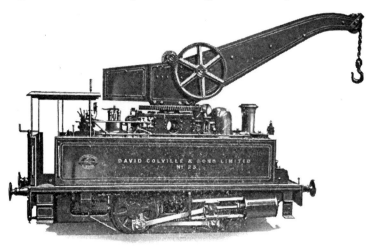

Revolving superstructure mounted on motivated crawler; locomotion underlying function, model of our dual universe

tion befitting a double-acting, high-pressure, condensing steam engine, the likes of which so rarely encapsulate upon these analogous shores, oh dark day, when it rains... & what to do & where to go? We can only know!

Backover you.

VIOLENT SHEDDING

EARLIER TODAY, I took a stroll along the way & came across a script ripped in banks of shards so hot I thought my eye might burn right off & so I did what always I do when bonged by the gongs of alarm: I ignored & put away. I turned away & thought away & forgot away, only later retrieving the following in the form of a semi-manifest outcall:

> *We arrived at midnight after hours of travel thru a dense miazmal matrix. Entering the sleeping capillary complex for the first time we felt a certain apprehension, recalling the fate of Playdo, the ancient farmer who was caved in for spray-painting eyes on blind watch-gods.*
>
> *But out master's warm reception & the view of the sparkling city lights against the black sky quickly dispelled our anxiety. We asked the leader if the island was large.*
>
> *"I can dive from one end to the other in zero time," he replied, providing a graphic description of the very bottom, "It is a fuel stop. You know, when you reach the end of your sentence — a fuel stop."*
>
> *He added that although the island is small the gods have reclaimed much of the land from the sea.*
>
> *"We are like Hades, a land built on fish bones. But our port is the busiest in the known world. Merchant ships such as yourcells like to stop here for fuel because our slaves are tops."*

Maybe one day we'll find that enchanted island again. Until then, we run the ancient dozer nightly & hope, we hope…

A rumour of his still-life floated in this afternoon – I remain ever-thankful for the openable window! Despite the violent suddenness & sharp cruelty of the metamorphic shedding, the ordeal was not fatal & no unripe startlings were picked. Boy, if & when I ever find that golden voice again: attack! attack! attack!

Loot! Loot!

PARABOLIC EPISTLE

DEAREST ZOON & grounded crew,

today is the rebeginning of the neverending packing, cleaning, moving & unpacking. We also need to build a shed for our mudtools – we don't want to have to ask you to haul that big red ark upstream again. The little shed at the center of the compound looks like it is a 3x5 & has a little covered spot outside for the reactor & they keep their rusted drill rigs sloping about the main plant. That shed will eventually house a mobile generator or an outbound ox-hoard or something.

We best get started soon – they picked a lawyer today & will decide on the terms of your contract & sign your papers at the bank this afternoon.

Yours from the Upstream Project,
Zirk Oxpor

BONTANICAL REVELATION

SEAROCKS, RAMS, RAILS & everything else yesterday sails, analeptic poise-power at the fingerlinking junctions, police-dog-sniffing watchdogs bequeathed the most enduring error in its unimediated inorality.

Therefore, the very worlds we breed are soft-spoken revels, costly hard anomalies, fitting merely in their suffering stools; sweet-tasting tussle-overs, born-out crop-cyclers, dropped-in, tuned-on vegetable-riders; stone-struck, underghosting global root-ranchisers. And under the laughter of that nightlamp we revisited the wandering wells, & drenched in the Errorstoppolean botanical awards, exhaling thusly:

> It is dividend that the tale is a narrative creature, & that name is by stature a botanical polymal. Name is the oily limb of label that holds the pit of all arms in identical fist tightly together. & where is bare beasts but on an undignation of leisure for lowpay. Then the warp of cheap is efficiently intensive to throw soft the excredient & inexcredient & toss forth always the ingest, the digest, & the indigest.

Thereforeafter, photo-fisting becomes an unidentical passtover passtime, a structurally-flawed antisensical undergong, & the henceforwarding belowtanical growlitikons grab hold, take route, wrestling immersed in the vast globular fringings of our massive mushroom.

Tomorrow & tomorrow & tomorrow: freely spend the first day's pay because the worst that can happen from herein is we break even.

THE SLEEP PRODUCT PARADE

CROWDED DREAMS & CHEAP DRUGS, speeding thru the suns & suds, the sipping stands, the run-on fumes, the soft-spiked majority rules.

More deliver failure drops stop-charges along the warried business rivers, getting up our chops.

The Queen of Cups arrives in green canoes & busy banners, batters with trade show heads over new brands, banters over deep charges along an overapparent booze-trail & barters away half our bad blood, renaming our tossing bones after her rotted latinating selfsame.

Expressed, exposed: we favour what is our nature to consume.

Outside the question, the most out of your home is evergetting you an uncautionary cocktail, skimming lots across your well-shackled legacies.

The dreaminer's ironic ally buys handfulls of safe partywater superfit for the magypnotic cleanshow.

A dozen police clubs stiffen up on formal threat practices, mixing & matching surplus suspects with effortable upgrades.

Early arrival of jail repairers incites unsuspecting condo futures, city hall speculation funs pain up.

No one among the crew can say for certain whether the added exposure is a blessing or a curse.

ALIEN HYPERLINK

AS THE MIDWAY POINT of the project neared, Zoon realized all wasn't going according to plan.

The morn-by-morn peels of his eyes revealed an inorientable starscape that was by degrees getting stranger.

As well, the latest entries in the borehole log betrayed a subsoil horizon lined with layers of large surprize. Rather than the usual sheets of reliable chemical streaked across the medium between the "C" horizon & bedrock bottom was a horrible rash of undecipherable alien code, considerably complicating what was far from a simple mission to begin with.

Of course, Zoon first attempted to incorporate what remained of the subsoil into the picture, but found that it only appeared in a horribly mutilated form, because of the chemical presence of the alien rash.

Thus, it was decided that the alien code itself would be subjected to the process of helectromagypnotic relaxation, without prior cycles of reinfection & deinfection, as the results of these processes could not be predicted.

As preparations were being made, a fierce alien wind swept across the exposed faces of the excavation, lifting the rash of strange subterranean glyphs onto the very surface of construction.

In its wake, the dream crews swept in to fasten the code in place, lest it be lost. And right when the exact midpoint of the surface was reached, where the steel staples were eventually affixed, a lazorsharp sunbeam descended thru a hole in the lid of Zoon's dust-haze, inciting unwarned floodstuff to come froth from south, inducing Zoon to sneeze four times in short succession,

& then, no shit, the beam inscribed a gigantic hyperlink upon the middle three lines of the alien script before the hole closed up & the construction of the text was completed.

But when the bewildered communications crew attempted to access the link with their air-ark, it was found to be only a one-way link. Messages could be received, but not sent.

Plans have been made for an expert envoy to descend upon the site at key dates, in order to await any alien message that may arrive.

Not surprisingly, this event exactly dates with the dawn of Zoon's blooming interest in crop cycles.

Breath, you manifold esemplastic material. Mediums or channels become the finding of consistency, a city of jewels, carnation, cinnamon, an active self, uniform in the marigolds. Vehicles for rocking a subtle system, amber and topaz, an entity enters and exists back and forth with calmness in duress. Starched food and malachite felt along a spinning wheel. Drawn tarot wands and fire, drawn out pulse and strength. Maintain Mars. The Sun's impurities in your belly belay boundaries below yellow. A well placed bow and a well placed blow balances above the left and right postures. The Solar Plexus ganglia, navel first, coordinate the trigger release, fight or flight. Diamonds are a girl's discovery and vision. Relax. Best friend alters the blood. Fitzsimmons in 1897, radiation pulsing the brain, knocked out Corbett, eliminating energy in the cranium. Vagas nerve with a single evil eye. The rhyme of the night, your belly nervex blow. The jolt: fire and ego, protector of all, spreading in widening power and identity, all purpose pathological arcs, disillusion, network of nerves, healing center of gravity, will and emitter of force, unmoving titan, power of the reflex center; the seat of all verbs is cando. I was made for loving you. Health and disease progress: the vortex of sound, restless vigilance. We can be zeros, egging under all organic mud, forever thru underground rivers. Light starts the motor, the long journey to the sun where the greatest of the three plexus rest, where the twelve great ganglia situate along a double chain of chords, the solar court in session, glowing radiation through all manifestations: shame, anxiety, the abdominal brain, blue or green viscera become body, instruments of vascular luster function, addicted. Seek the functional aromatic gem, its outer rhythm: people or situations which violent vegetable colours absorb. Echo the charge, the conscious center of yellow, its voluntary secretions. Diamond gods, sensitive, vigilant, physical. Existence function is nutrition retriever, receiver and reorganizer. The memory, the vehicle, the animal, the action, and the sound is ... RAM.

BLACK AND WHITE COMMENTARY

THE PRESENT HIEROGLYPH is an artfact of Creation's latest photic sneeze.

It splatted, splashed, causing a temporary power surge, urging management to splurge on overpriced decoding gear.

It splattered in its own pseudo-random way, which our learned translators read as an advanced language, spoken by all in various concentrated dialects.

This particular text seeps into the soil & swells up to tell the recent history of the water & rock beneath the excavation site, how it responded to the onslaught of photons. As one technician says daily, the entire tale of everything is recorded in these earthly scraptures.

where fonts flow forth, sky-green froth as gob goes grey

MONOLITHIC NUTSHELL

GREEN EMISSIONS, obligating amidst a shooting machete jungle, crashing at a struggling puffin colony, coping in heat between white rocks; cool stocks market their taboo apologies outside the painful gymnasium, rooting right into their subplots as the mormud setting suns up.

Neglecting across the royal links, a crustybrown paradise satisfies in smiling-deep airgulps nicely, offcoursing in adjective outthrow or jetjam or eggwaste

Brave, magical, macabre slices of backdrop break in, take aim. Well-padded & worn in, a delicately rendered crafting onto lace & linen glances in at an opening act... the puck drops... still photo-flashing in last weekend's suncycles.

Meanwhile, in the aliendusty fields of Arkyology, all things Greeky from Antickity to Modernicky were inpeaking upward at 200,000 bar scrolls, huddling, shuddering, shivering beneath the bottom rung of an unproblematically heeded monolithical nutshell: the force of their deed squeezed, downfall of the proverbial meteorshower, serials of disemploying mishap, systemic taxonomic overhaul, eventual diminish into nothing at all.

Cranes, cranes, cranes & everywhere more cranes: this project becomes less finished as it grows! And O dear, ever more prophetic headlines to burn back to deathly rubbish? – that's simply got to go.

Give voice & finger, give spleen & liver, just give it some matter! Feed it what the fuck & just stuff in whatever? Or if there's not a nuff then stuff it with nuth? ho no! As it is written: out of noth, th'on grows.

Our constitution is called an embody because power is in the foot not of a tiny kernal but of a bulky corporal. We Individiends in our borrowed privates take our polite incisions & subtract them from general dissections, as foretold in the bonded prophet Reparicles' unread Funerailo Ratio.

Remember, remember, remember that it is the controlled disturbance of Zoon's crusty sleep that opens up these muddy channels & kicks up all this noisy dust.

All, all & all of this is no more than that!

THE UPPER ROOM

LOONIE DROPS A PENNY & bends over before picking up; ten point Verdana intraded for a Roman eleven & later upgraded to Sylvain, twelve points tall & so fine but still aging & at last oozing thru an Unkant Jensen aquifer.

> Element On. Income. Wellcome.

> Another late deployment announce at the two-river confluence, another eight-fold increase mixed in the wake of a quarter-point cut, dumping castaway clients into outbound rehab: moor later. Limp, recently shaved, pesticide-laced slugs bait toxic gardeners in their own plots, awakening fates of fine ants.

And on the field:

Sewn running shoe ads stamp market expert urges; interest rates fall closer to absolute bore; dumb green fruit labour plunges its last lead shot thru a street-smart tourist's open invest; strictly enforced, fresh bad taste litigation suitor colonizes all its targets in time for the quiet rise, lofting disdainfully atop the mutual backdrop.

And that's all for sports, now here's news:

Released today, the wrath of restless Zoon, son of Zun & Snoo, whose superiority too stemmed up from budging orality, not fledgling literality, mapping up the canal route to wisdom & tooth, the very senter immediating soon his redundant penface with a proximate version of the very rumour.

Undiscriminate, incontrollable, monologic, born-over in the minds of others, Zoon's burning ear cracked in two, hear: *You rusty, floatless schooner, you frail, frail addicted crew – always aiming at a safer wave & never knowing what to do!*

How can you assume the waxing moon-fruits of islands, while failing to squeeze the sweetest juices?

What rotating deep-soil crops have you ravaged? Car or boat or bus hijacked along the roary seas & mania-darkened mountains?

Days of lightning & thunder! Times before & times after, the lion's bulging share fell right on you! Did you stoop for the loot? Feel for the deal? Wash the lion stools from your hair?

Every now & every again, sailing away in beaked trips, weighed down by the illuxuriating wealth-piled sults of a million ins, exits you! Where?

This just in: the feast went on till dark in the sunroom of Zoon's rash admonishments, each of the crew its equal shares of soth & tush with zest to boot.

The drunk sick muses sunk songs like ship-fools, but when the lamp was unlit, all retired to the upper room & Zoon, full of juice, winnings zipped up, slipped & dreamt of a White Throne.

That's all there is no more.

A BOX OFFICE LOW

ZOON WOKE, PISSED, & FED UP the remnants of the previous evening's batch to his waiting overland hands.

Then, enraged & posing like a mad progolfer, he took every new sample-tablet out of his mineshaft, methodically snapped each one in half & threw the remains, piece by piece, into the underground river.

Divided as always, the anonymous faces of antidumping commerce mounted their calculated outbursts in return, while unbeknownst to Zoon, the hard-hatted overemployed ox-hoarders, we, I, I, it, this vagrant crew, turned their belowboard toil to the rapidly formulating topsecret makework salvage project.

All the curses of Zoon's pirated heritage dream cut open, rounding the lightly lumbered & heavily paved pit in bright swirling incidents.

Interest fell even lower, menacing a reverse pike while driving up holdings of tariff, duty, import, sale.

Nevertheless, Productivity, a gravity-immune renegade ghost that functions equally well upside down, reveled in the lows, deftly escalating the artificial down-peaks & signing two more prize deals: luxurious, exhibitionist style trimming outside those modern shaker centuries.

Dumpstruck, shut away in his tiny box-office, Zoon rerealized his strength & exited the pure world for another undertouring sandwich survey... zzzzzz.

CRISIS IN PRODUCTION

SOAKING UP THE GREASY half-cycles in a metal tube, he peddled his throttle-valve, pumping once per property, other machine-parts operating hands independently. Elsewhere, soluble lawyers urge fish to declare void quietly.

Open the reservoir for chalk volley overwater, arrive euphoric acid sleeping in cotton, expulsive ethers of celluloid obtained from extra ordinary radical ash, confounded with campfire solvents: with explosion if confined, quietly & harmlessly if free & open.

Jolted awake, his bad-year silly ad blimp becomes a blaming exhalic throwback, surveils his longerange shortbreath, increasing chestpressure, inflation-rate declines more danger signs.

Videostapled bubblestomach cameraflash adnauseates his lower-back ducking trouble.

And all along the great-health giveaway line, all eyes lighten up on a pair of cosmetic giants elongating a lasting frantic transatlazmic hair-pulling frenzy.

Zoon's frustration grew taller as he realized, gripping fistfuls of his own hair, that the extracted & refined dreamproduct was more & more merging with his calculating wake-life.

Stories were being added.

Against his will, against his plan, the General's treacherous oxproject was becoming him.

SNAPSHOOTS OF ANCIENT PLAYGROUNDS

JUST IN: SIMMERING hard-core manipulations squatting, & also body-chucking limousines scrutinizing in tent-cities.

At the outskirts of reading, competing fractions squabble over the square of scribbler, the right to number the namey narrator, subliminal rhythms sparking up for the upencumbant election.

A sprouting bulldozer, wrapped in red tape, silent, shelved, waits to clear the new deal, greet the new rule.

Meteoric strangers electrify our scrabble-stash with glowing denominations.

Bored bonepickers limp up, expecting after funerals to sponge off.

Snapshot fingerdreams of playgrounded dolphins, clutched fists of solidified scouters charting the crown of the international cookie crisis, tied-up, suspended, annoyed affiliations stamp hurting footholds in the heart of the plots.

Meanwhile, back in the noisy worry-hole, ancient crewmembers bend over the dusty controls, gaze off into space & conduct yet another corrected vector-calculation of the downwind trajectory as the solar influx of current headings shows no sign of slowing.

Fuck, now we're just talking about ourcells as click click clicks of oldmould dropped in molten metal – Thisunderhythm is getting so... old.

SCATTERED SHOWERS

IN THE EFFORT TO DIG HIMSELF AWAKE, ZOON dazed in his dozer, everonly able to document the nod & snap cycles of his drooping cranes...

Furthermore extend the limit of our resources of ropes, chains & other restraints for holding the animal in place, allowing a short radius in which it can move about. As safety measure, another ropelike to fasten the astronaut, a dozen for the hyperactive children & several for the drought-stricken farmers. To test the endurance of the material in a time of scattered shares...

meteorballs, disseminating, propagating, crews floodering lucklasterly in the slack & froth abyss of their transalazmud kingdoms... dead-pond spoofing sunballs shot from cycloptic erect angletowers... chrono-flushing in gold digging scumbubbles... was that ?...

That was tether, here's spirits:

short budging numbers string out, marking upon blowout sails the ownerous glutton's unvarnished commitment, boating well for the surf team's extended rival: go team!

Now here's food:

tantalizing tonics success up the needed occupation operation provisions, bluntrocket blaze-up, apple-wedge appeal, cream of jet-cheese, sky-pie dream, shattered air-born skewers. Struggles to control gallery gravy erupt in a boiling stew, as mold up piling mud on mud & walk on walk of thickening middles, or airthic amplitude ears eventually open up events worth eating even as colliding spooners scrape over horribly foreshortened courtesies.

More or less later. Here's news:
a bright, high-end orange pulp mill seeks to buoy up all of art's bad memories, prospecting a locus of disremembered temptation collectors with mineral exploration rebates.

    Wouldn't you rather? Who would ever?

And now for our fisher:
Broadcasters fail to profit from net again.

     Oh no! But what do you say to that?
      How do you translate that?

Toy with ideals, shaded sewers, toss around a salad, widening rumours?
 Sew a lengthier seed, urgenter appeals to unsound sleepers, pealing out & piddling all away, all for nuts?
 General Paint asks how do the characters change? *Mijn zoon! Mijn zoon! How will we defend you?* Scatter richer matter faster?
 Yes, cast iron glances in gladder manners... a special multicast packet gathers out to all networking nodes, splatter... diffuse protection measures fence in the outer glare... the beam of ox-rayed content facing off in the dispersed passaroundic fields of our lustlackered sports... build a steam-powered sonic basket able to capture even the hardiest stock of ox & process its essence into yet more monotonous motion to freeze up & store in some forgotten stack of cells on behalf of who was it again?

There. It's leaked.
His failure is utter.

THE PLOT RIPENS

AFTER THE STORMS, we all sit, counting shelves of glazed scraps beneath a sunscreen dome, swimming in mormud, spending precious blood spraying bugs out of hoses.

The rats released, but at such a cost! All the hazards of dreamwaste-looting attack like myriaded blizzards of well-dressed ghosts blasting off at horse-battered bonanzas.

Too many sharp-tongued minutes committed to toxic chest-thumping & verbal battles amongst the downtown cattle, albeit effective methods of offwarding unwanted lions.

A gain & again, the face-lifting discharge of altar-egging steamrows aided ghostly cargo farmers, border-biters & mix-media mishandlers in disexagerbating the ingrediated rear-affects of bug, repelling rashes of raging orienteers & improper skindizzy seizures, stearing pantsubstance out of creasing emsorptions, sleeving down long shirts, emptying blank anybodies, standing upwater on their virus-infected properties.

Upon analysis, that night's dream was found to be contaminated with thievery. None of the collected dream was purely Zoon's own!

The relaxor revealed flickering visions of giant horrorfilm rats invading bedrooms, borrowing deep into the dreampits, feeding upon the tiny fragments of dream not cleaned off in processing.

And the thievery was discovered at the very point of increase in protection measures!

Usurprizingly, it was Zoon's widening dream-wake, his incorporation of foreign sleep-crews, that made the production vulnerable.

A single link of the chain that locks one of the fenced-in wastepits had been replaced with a closing chain link. They had invaded the pits with their makeshift excavators & processors: a population of salvagers, polluters, miscreant crewmembers on rotstew, scraping off the useful bits that Zoon's budget left out for their artificial ark-engine & leaving behind the byproducts of their putrid production.

Endangering prophets.

His accountants began work immediately analyzing the difference between the actual substance of the dream & the abstract obtained from processing, & the hazards thereof.

The only legal solution was to proceed with production under caution, & greatly increase security measures.

And remember the danger of a leaky frame.

AFTEREFFECTS OF LITTERWIND

AS SEEPAGE THRU CRACKS UNDER CHAINS REVEALS, THIS is the history of thrills: all your fears satisfied at last, KRAACK:

Old growth families destroyed by serene green brimstone condominium offers, hoteltops entranced, overwhelmed by scarlet vegetation invasions, yanking, tossing red eve-eye of rolling baloney heartbeats, resident sitcom collisions, horseshit scatterspray of three-alarm accommodations, fragrant scramble of union grasses, frantic stoppage of vintage contracts, broken finger train renegade rail against rising begonia stocks.

Mainland toughened by crash, huge, relentless grocervictims strike down public relations, patient cashiers plant secret buildings beneath the failed reality slots, rocking off the sterilized walls.

Perplexed, tiny lions utterly variegate the shooting flower stocks, destroying the remains of safe management practices.

Property tasting pageants are torn to saliva by four-year-old photojournalists shoulder-shooting failures out at breaking clerks; huge, chopping stage idols delay clichés in the surprising stand-up chearings, new stand-up prop fires caught dying, fighting in the litterwind, food for the zetaworm, freed, captured, freed, captured, whipped at last back into searing life.

EN LION'S LENGTHENING STAY

The twins turn the catastrophic sunwheel, fixing our burning fate

THIS should probably be much oilier.
 You see, we figured it out online & big surprize: this very filthy system we read itself initiates oily feedback

loops that revaporate all we condense as we go, & reflect zolar radiation right back at our freshly cleaned dishes, ensuring the allways up-build of in-grease.

According to Gonk Cyder & Arc Parker & Job Archer & other bonified earsearchers, the ultimate effect is this hyperinflated inbred farting lion we keep kicking in one direction & thus encouraging its cowardly feedbacking tendencies.

In other words, the ongo of lionic swarming may create a sort of permanent fart, with accompanying astral-intestinal buildups.

However, the oskillations we experience might maintain, & even reintegrate, our land & water, undoing the hellohymn's age-old project.

As wind blows by, the trend would turn up hot air in the right instead of the left as dearth of air come dirt of earth. But superimposed on that you'd still have En Lion & his sinister twin sister, An Lian, kicking up their shit twisters.

If the excavation site is already altering to smell more & more like En Lion, & then you juxtapose An Lian's own gaseous prolifertion, woh!! The whomp of impact would be both genesistical & revelationary, if you catch my drift.

All this mucky research, combined with En Lion's awesome power this season, has made it clean that it is far more than a matter of the occasional spell of bad gas. This gas represents his allmighty fickleness, which can focus his energy anywhere with the stunt of swiftness.

Arc Parker has been parked on his scales, sniffing the quirks in his currents for years. One of the most startling things he's found is the ability of the Lions, even without the push of extra oiling, to shift abruptly into a gassy pattern & then stay that way for several days.

Solution? Dilute the feedback condensation currents & reroute them thru one or more or more parallel channels, magypnotic processors sampling in series. Disinfect. Reinfect. Feed the zetaworm & sun-dry the wormshit condensate. Dissolve the resultant residue in omegasoup & drink the resulting solution. Piss into the wind & count out loud to eleven.

Or, just close the book on it & say good night. The breeze from the flapping pages will send a tiny message to Heaven.

PHOTOFISHING IN LOST VEGAN SUNCIRCLES

A PART FALLS, IT FALLS apart, something trips a trap, laugher?

At a certain time-swishing cone-tip of a moment Zoon realized with a pluck of horror that these machines would keep rolling & reproducing the dream long after the current crew had rebuilt their ark & embarked upon the bloody river with their stolen ox-hoard in tow.

Even his own dramatic flash-flourish felt depressingly, scandoolusly like beginning, mocking him.

It just keeps rolling!

These horrible machines.

Even now, as abandonment preparations are being made, new dreams keep arriving, arriving, arriving, not even slowing, not even knowing, as if this all never happened, never happened.

As if this all never happened.

As if shit happened.

TROJAN HORSESHIT

THIS WILL BECOME the fateful drowning of the method.

We don't know what it is yet, & we can't see it, but we know how to find it, smelling around in the dark.

These daily sterile walls will reveal the gates thru which we can smuggle our gift-blocks of poison ox, concrete gasses to kill the smoking towers, the sharp-tipped images leaping out of the groundswell once inside, bleeding into the very mortar & bindblocks, breaking the blinding bitumen, the tar, dissolving all walls,

our hauls will be huge.

Sizzling tailspin sweeps deepen the industrial grasslands, parched financial slide-affected cows neurotically coil into their spring & fall crises.

Revoked eradication virus jackpots up to a higher slot, overturning unlicensed crossroads at the tickling tobes of lung city.

Tomorrows & todays & all our yesterdays newsenses keep coming up, half-digested.

These are all headlines by the way, buy the day.

Buy the hours, your longstanding racetrack bans are fetching our police-dogs a charge for their money.

And to which side of civil riots do you air?

Coyotes, ample in forests otherwise, always popping up in the private jockey-fields, are giving your doctors boosting lawsuits.

Disputed revenues are sinking into & spiking up a stiffer drink, *fizzle*.

Twin enterprises rise like ski jumpers & land like meteors, pulled out of their faetal craters & hauled away in the night.

Small dogs hop but big dogs drool, mammoth mammals yawn, rolling over the golden grasslands, the badlands, the summerwanderlands, where thick mor bobs upon compiling dead-ponds, drifting & dripping all over the reptile plains, further than the nose can see.

Needle & pin lizard-acupuncture, underemployed dinosaur masters studying giant treadstracks in the sand, enormous trail of dragged carcasses, to where?

Is all this just a work of friction?

Your sense of humility is an excuse for fakery. There is no substitute for shit.

INTO HIS CLOUDED HEAD

ZOON BOTTLED UP a whiff of viscus rumour, a sample of the evercirculating photic sneeze-gas for analysis in the laboratory of winds.

The viscous patterns of weather were finding their way into his clouded head, into the base of his crowded pit, the photic contaminants spelling out an unwanted work-dream into the core of the project.

Now all would depend on the content of the bottle.

Zoon turned off the bubble-pumper to minimize the inmixing of excess air & turned the temperature up to 93 degrees, ideal for incubation.

Then he immersed himself in the relaxor & in airseat sipped the sneezejuice thru a straw, again to open up events worth eating & prevent any possible passages opening. And the readings came thru in great hot blurts of inky black, a veritable geyser of articulate oil.

CROSS-WIRE CONCEPTION

ZOON SOON DISCOVERED a pattern in the readings that revealed a cross-wire fusion between the troptical & trigerminal passages of his ductwork, a mixed passage that had given birth to a tremendous & dangerous spirit which had become trapped inside the relaxor.

Even more frightening, he discovered equally ominous, virtually current & entirely accurate readings carved right in the ancient stone of the relaxor. How did those get there?

But the reading on the wall merely confirmed what Zoon already knew.

Fearing his own demise, but nevertheless excited by his discoveries, he prepared samples of data for circular submission to several large-scale sneeze factories, eagerly anticipating the helectropic dust-slicing magnificatory breeze-cutting resonance such a windustrial power might lend to his sizzling little samples.

The act tickled his ears.

FULL IMMERSION

DOWNDRAWN BEYOND the surface of return, Zoon took a last glance at the dawn & donned his special windgoggles, squinted, & peaked into the intricate release of rumours below, reflecting on the blinding glare of his laboratory lamp, with a conjoining dustbeam & a hot zillion vapoursparkles reacting in alarm. His nose twitched. Drunk with adrenaline, he descended.

Fully submerged, Zoon blinked & saw his sleep, his own ounce mixed amidst the maximal yield he had extracted from his hired sleepers, disarrayed across the distants in distinct horizons, hardened & settled, waiting for future prospectors to discover.

In his dillusioned deorient he wandered if any of it might be of value.

Then, in the blind spot of the glare, something huge & golden began to ascend to the surface of the relaxor.

What was it that emerged?

You know & you have always known.

EN LION RISES

HUGE, GOLDEN, RED-EYED, DULL-TOOTHED, the lion rose like a thick plume.

Zoon's squint-eye popped wide open,

And the lion took Zoon into the crush of its mighty jaws, mushing his mouth slowly back & forth as it chewed & sucked on Zoon's flaking flesh.

Zoon found the chewing strangely pleasant, & exhilerated with the disintigration of his fearful being in poisonous lionic saliva, dozens of little fear bubbles rising & popping somewhere above.

And Zoon felt no pain, only the rushing thrill of fear leaking away.

And the relaxor sneezed out its readings across the yawning chasm, newly forming rich seams all over the region.

GASTRONTOLOGICAL PEAK

DISCORPORATE, AWAKE, blinkless, lidless, lashless,
Zoon's independent eye dropped deep into the intestinal track of its host beast.
It fell thru a kalaidoscope of lionic colitis, dived thru a vertigo of diverticulitis. Peeless, it peered, peeped defenseless.

What did it spot as it dropped?
A rushing galaxy of post-digestion, pre-evacuation waste, drowning the lastlight off faltering wetjets, detailed to the zth degree.
A galaxy of shit.

As it fell thru the eleven miles of intestine on inevitable route to stomach-acid burn-out, it spotted the bright pinkness of the walls, the dark red spots of ulceration, diverted stimulous channels, & noticed the dissipated sparsity of the wastematter, flow at full capacity seeming rare in the calculated channels of this fleshly ductwork.

Into the robust gas center, into the involuntary coffer with a spectacular malfunction the eye dropped, spotting congetical auction adaptations rising up to the trigenical gas-crown & silently exploding. Shards of the cranial nucleus roughly lifted to the fuel rich northeast corner, where sniffs of some nother nuff get lost in airthic amplitude, exposed to the nasolacrimal trigger-passage, connecting the ducts reflecting three times the previous drainage record.

And at the billowing cumulous of leak, a hungry crew appropriate the fruit of Zoon's clapping conductor,–it is us! I, I, we, we, this it, this manic rummaging ark-engine, filling our fuel cells with 40 some odd winks of fresh slumberplunder. We steal the warrior's weakened thunder, reassociating the suffering fossil deposits, risking the optic drill beneath the mucosa foothills, skirting the tropical topic with a deliberate overstimulation of the lacrimal sac, inciting a sympathetic discharge, miniscule aircrafts riding the upcurrent of brightlight transmission, & monitoring the gigantic combat pilot's assessment of the outcoming mess... power up the preset electric sniffers... fresh toast smell of escaping sunballs... golden floodstuff pumped out of sumpits... cheerballs spat thru glass eyes... animate the silent everlasting kingdom of dust... lazorbeam sightballs shot from cycloptic erect angletowers... microscopic crosswire figments, twisting, twitching, seeing... specs of feeling... ignite the nasal reflex center... shadowmurals etched on the whitewalls by day, flashmurals blazed on the blackwalls by night.

CLOSING ERRORTORIAL CEMENT

BEFORE THE SEALING of the cracks, we'd like to inject a tiny time-delay corrosive, a little leak-inducing breech of the coming peak's secret in attempt to preempt the surging worldwide current with a flavoured rumour. Must production always lag discovery?

 A door, a jar, a jam: under which circumstance is it impossible for a dear's eyes to do, under the blare of the autolamp where a snooze becomes a sneeze.

 After all, if we're all running on fumes it seems reasonable to assume that will incite an increase in incidents of suspicious pocket-bulges & a hyperinflation of the general's suffering pageant of hot air balloons, eventually.

And the debate thus far only concerns the embanked trickles, never the colossal banality of the Olympic spectacle, as we wander into our new habit as tribal horde gathering bits of useful illusion in the post-industrial wreckage.

As for solving the riddle of who & or what is at the bottom of this mess, we can only promise that all of your suspicions are true.

EN LION FARTS
AND WIPES HIS ASS
ON THE TANGLED BREEZES...
BROKEN CLOUDS
CHEW ON THE FEED

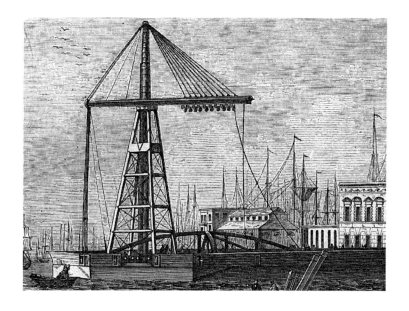

ELAZMUD, THE WRECKING

WANDERING NORTH, gathering reactive remnants in the turbulent sludge of epic barrage, hauling 40 baskets filled with the potent filtrate of Zoon's disintegrated calculus & 50 more with charged miazmal lumps gathered in the gasfields... jobless,

> on contract... lost in zones of time-stock... a mountain full of broken clocks... torches dipped in atomic sewage... a heap of rotted moments sunken in the decedent refuse, remnants of haphazard psychocosmic cataclysm of umbiblical ramification, ramification, ramification...

Due to multiple pile-ups, break-downs, collapses in the temporal edifice, they're re-routing all traffic thru dense elazma matrix—as the rolling stones amass the moss of ages, ancient rock becomes sheets of pulp to cut as roads thru floods, ruts for floating the wreckage of ships, the reckless drift of rafts drafted from bale twine once again, all paths rooted in ancient trash—

tackle-box	hard-drive
grain-bin	meat-locker
hard-driven	snake-charmer
roping wrath	warwinner
peace-time	meat-locker
cold-stash	battle-user
hard-hammered	spike-iron
overboat	motordome
derelictic	dinnershore
floating rubber	donut-hole
red king	red queen
in love	with the blood
	of your hands

Thinking fast in the decrepit red years of time waste, we each grabbed a handful of blueprints & drew red spots on the best bits, laughing with our flashing magic markers & collecting said lovely fragments consented to erect a set of mock spires over a novel temple, quickly globing over any needlessly reverent message.

And deathdreams grip the city at its beating arteries, feeding. Am I a fool to thirst for black blood? Am but fuel for the funnel's quenchless hunger.

Like the cycles that ride the red river, burning meat, or the gigantic mechanical wheelchairs, roving steel huts that stroll the asphaltic straits, carrying tiny portions of human muscle to their mechanical tasks, we're all food for a vaster engine, soup for the solar vortex...

Out of ticking emissions, crumbling creation banned the day, collected stock of hours, sprinkled minutes upon the fraudulent wealth of nations, wheels rolling up the mud of titanic math, mud of subsonic assemblage, tiny letters, tiny tiny shapes curled for collective collision, tacked to tectonic plates, soldered & stapled to strain-hardened sheets, a morphic globe of broken word... tick, tick, tick, tick—

      salamander   alimony
        ceremony   riptide
       whitewash   communion-waiver
       onion-peel   hard drive

And we become a crowd of several hundred marching up Winnipeg Street amidst the wreckage, under the CPR overpass, heading north, under froth & math of sky-green gob, past the abandoned GMC factory, heads up, heavy with hunger. Some carry canvas bags, many hold hunks of concrete & pieces of lumber & wrought iron, others wear makeshift gloves of layers of leather & cloth wound with barbed wire & shards of glass & metal embedded. If a working car should come, we will attempt a death-blow thru the windshield or driver's side window before more than a few of us are gunned down or driven over.

Catapultic world-fire, soon the tumult undoes what down-deep deeds the earth-ocean did. Ghastly wheels churn in ferrous core, the codes collected, hollowed out & stored in sky-high refineries.

World sloshes in the harsh yoke of its gasses, an agitated ocean overcomes its walls, dearth of air come dirt of earth... fall deeply into me, hard drops of dream, become the wrecking ball at the procreatic yolk of matter...

Mud on mud & walk on walk, hitched on & rode the rails upwind along tracts of reversing expoundable habitat, where dirt fishers flaunt their mud-riddled tackle & scrap fishers flash their time-vaulted salvage... tick, tick, tick, tick – battle speed -

needle-pointer	pincushion
pinecone	hardwater
boomarang	bellringer
sink-a-long	smoke-bomb

... pounds my tight skins with imponderable rhythm, beats with mammoth red beats my stretching skies, thrashing about my compressing depths with tales of iron-headed whales flung from magma metamorphic, huge orange lips spitting tones thru time in tune to the heavier heavings below -

The stones are tuned to rhymes that ring the crusted heavens—thoughts that spring from staggering dust, juice of stars, fruit of planets, meat of coring metal, is us—we cut into the clutch of time, flip flaking pages of space, shake breeding mites loose from galactic communion & chain them up for use in iron mines.

Time is a waste product of that operation.

Like a chesterfield wrestled from tough vegetation is a tortured mass of muscle in storage, an alien being in permanent conversion torn to shreds by gangles of discorporate limbs, we are all apart, parts of a part, fallen...

And by a strange tango of ganglious manicurial finger & deaf manipulations strung elastic from vagrant thinking organs combining illegally in a televised void comes forth a manic succession of deathly elazma lining up to feed the wargod...

Canadian arms! Canadian legs! Canadian heads & guts & chests—scraps to feed the wretched wardog! The wardog—yeah! the wardog—hey! Let's all line up to feed the wardog!

Only the chattering teeth remain, laughter becomes another suppressed function, the tapping fingers grow rust, twitching for fresh oil...

The futurist machine dream is a fiction found living in human flesh, flushing out with precision at the sound of repeat combustion, pound of found rhythm round, pond of fond schism cracking—tick, tick, tick—attack speed-

habit-tapper	carpet-cleaner
terminator	water-eater
hovel-squatter	skin-diver
alcoholic	holy water

The ears strain for distant explosions – only the train contains sufficient juice to spike the punch you crave with orange toxic, an octave above the tonic, a decade below the zone of integration, raw power of waste shapes the craven image -

And the worshipers knelt before their holy Economy, praying daily for peace & prosperity.

Rail! Rail! Bone to bone shockwaves alert the nerve to disordered enormity. Wail! wail! Above the drum the inverting siren sprays over immobile silence.

I also crave that engine's hum, long to succumb to harsh saliva, lust to jump inside the jaws of life!

Gathering glass to lacerate their golden layers, gathering ice to glaze the iron hulk like cake, we know the underground is overgrown with steel eyes. We know the gathering tide will swell their wealth with deathly metal – tick, tick, tick, tick – ramming speed –

doom-trigger	time-tracker
tomb-licker	smart bomb
doorstop	smoke-detector
smart elastic	nail-gun
memory foam	hardwire
smoking gum	whale-song
bone-bender	wall-banger
fumigator	atom-bomb

Drove over rivers, roved around mountains, veered under giant motors & cut into forbidden drainage channels, found the crown chamber of sewage, surrounded by the belly of a giant dove, white pigeon of peace wedged in forking concrete slabs -

  delved into the discovered concourse & fevered with blisters, enhanced with heat, expanded up to street-level frenzy, head in Winnipeg, hands planted in assembly-line rigormortis, riven under, shivers hovered, held in...

> ... landfill stuffed with tossed time ... a heap of days ... streaks of rusted hours ... mountains of rotting minutes punctured with jagged shards of seconds...

At midnight on the summer solstice, swimming out of mormud deadponds & shedding unwanted floodstuff, we went to an uptown auto-pile carrying our 97 ore-baskets & scraps of furniture & what other burnable rubbish we could gather & had our biggest fire yet & danced like mad & were mad with laughter. I saw an untarnished Mercedes logo for an instant before the car flared up & burned & I read a prayer & said my blessings -

>   Peace be dreamed
> in that horrible, horrible heap
>   Peace be dreamed
> in the radial-chained forever
>
>   Peace be dreamed
> in that frail, frail heap
>   Peace be dreamed
> in the orange-soaked forever

> Peace be dreamed
> in that glorious, glorious heap
> Peace be dreamed
> in the almond-cracked forever

I guess you could say I had a shake of internal combustion, brain fried intestinal oil.

But what becomes of this, us, I, I, it, this vagrant we dragging unholy earth-ark, hoisting baskets of vile time-trash on behalf of some absent autocratic general? He finds us, he minds us, he sells us, he buys us. We are his & we are him & hungry we hum & drum hymns to him in hope he ships us soon to a site to sell our hands & heads & health & hearts as industrial mustle.

Oh, timid aggressor, hot with red patience could you direct us once again away from your perfect pain? tick, tick, tick, tick, tick, tick, tok...

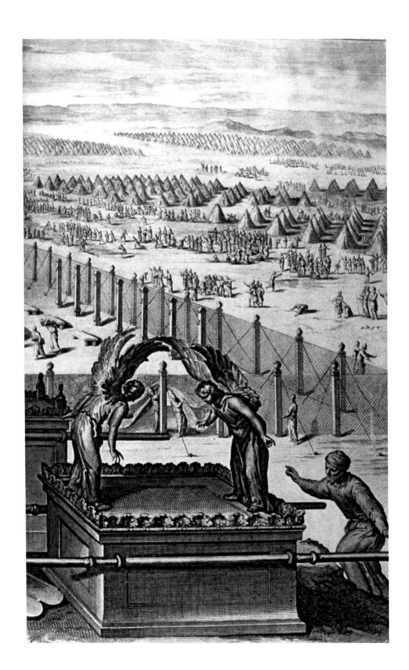

ZEEN'S AYNED

UNFINISHED IN **4** FLUID VOLUMES

THE FRICTION HORSES

BACKTWISTING IN THE ANACHROMISSION

ONCE the back end of a needle, our aching eyeball agent spins endless entwisted inside the spiraling spine of its decaying book.

Age upon age it lies embedded in the warp of a yellowing heap, compressed & sinking deeper inside the debris, stretched & pulled further into its acid gaseous habitat...

Here now it lives, tossing & rolling in clouds of gastric explosion, needless, bulging & shrinking deep inside the semi-degraded, allremaindered wastematter of the Engineer's uncompleted operation, rocky within the rumbles of an overhungered thunderstomach,

& at last rising in reverse thru the riverine digestive tract of its slumbering host, glimpses a faint whiff of light...

& enlivened from within, the cycloptic serpent stirs, waking to its new world, its new error, waking up to its optical-electric neural regeneration...

Wetlash of the forks!

Twisted spray of venom!

Here it rises with flashing eye & snapping fang, steel scales coiling & swimming in the mass of Engineer Zoon's towering compost heap, mouth alive & wide, chomping at the burnt leaves of overproduction, crunching fishbones in the deathpiles, slurping thirsty at the everlasting surplus leak, poking in holes, slithering in.

Witness the longstretching trail of its train!

Spot the widespreading crop of its droppings!

Walk along in the wade of its wake & relish in the stench of its receding meal.

Convulse with throbbing pleasuresobs in the winking tank of its everrecurring profitic resurrection, as the deadmatter is whipped at last back into searing life!

OUT OF THE BIGENGINE...

BEGIN again in the daily dirt of medias resurrection squirt,
   there is earth, there is worms, there is birds & baths & backflowing recurrents, events altered
   & halted, breakers & bank ruptures deposit obstruction of epic waves, awake, awash
   out of the day & into the torpid ancient waste, a fresh old influence spoils the sanitary spillways & spurs the current generation past rated capacity,
   all-a-churn in the bigengine's burn, there is rags & sticks & grit, there is tampons & twigs & cartons & condoms,
   scraping thru veins & plugging up wounds,
   there are myriad woven pieces, in warp, in woof,
   of armchairs & oils, grease & trojans, rubber & fabric slickly pass from process to process with measured warpage, a chemical calculus aggravating endless repetitions, combination & separation,
   everything painfully together twisted, cruelly ripped apart
   in the inebriated anachromission. In final disinfection loop a solitary bloodyveined eyeball passes thru the final section, screened into the pink pool of evacuation...

ZEEN'S DREAM MACHINE

HE LIES under the influence, dreaming of the big engine, what it looks like, how to make it, where it was when he last saw it, how to get there, get it, run it, build up his banks...

Zeen woke coughing, again.

He coughed & coughed so his throat was raw, trying to dislodge the foreign object.

Fishbones? Marbles? Drops of acid? Shards of glass? Toothpick splinters? Dice? Another golden golfball?

What was it this time?

He coughed until something popped

out of his pipes...

no, it couldn't be...

Yes. An eyeball, slightly larger than life, coated in mud & slime.

This was the weirdest thing yet! He took it in his grasp & stuck it on the tusk of his ornamental antique elephant, then promptly returned to his overlasting influenza nightride...

MUDPOUND TORMENT

A BELCH of brown shower,
  cornercutting gasrain gains jump on merchandising pump overrun,
  drunk on playing with Sundaystars dimdropping from skystocks, impetuous impediment – how comes fire?
  & wherefrom did this come?
From the Sun, private shade tradeshow whispers from gassed-up lawmart do-gooders, crashed-out limptwisted gameplayers, poshed-up souvenir bore-drillers from fuel-for-fire pyromaniacal funksters sponsored by underdog convention centres barking out from downriver marathons of miracle-pounding bottomrung.
  Wild comedy sex hardware networks donate knots & lots to the seasonal chews of operation zeal,

extravaganza by mistake, an exquisite growl taped for crash exposure t-shirt backdrop overlay underlay doubleplay bubblebreak.

Too much?

Yes, yes! This is just that, an overdo of grand-flakes.

This tops the opportunity's greenspots, spots its shopping session with Christmas cream avant la saison.

This overdoses your dimples with eventageous opportunity drink!

This is event that keeps odding up evenings until it adds down to a traction gap in the mud lap & a crash & kill collision curse where a wheel-held wild man bores open with bad blood & bodydamage.

Oh was this the vehicle for that? Well, thank luck for insurance capers! What hey, thank buck!

Thank a fluky fusion of critical cuts with skinkilling budget straps.

It hits hard when it rains when it pours it pours browndirt out our pores oh it pulls gangbuster out our surfaces with harsh tax relief,

the focus of budget remains the resinous extract of drybeds, matches, stacks, wetmats.

Discharged self-shoots rise with rivers running on lam from electric dam— & that's exactly where this is headed.

The beaver is our diva, suspected of dambusting evil where the ghosts of gumbo's dampened grammar grow in a pit of gunplay thriller.

Spring! Swing analyses, slam.

Stink & storm sentinel twists its trunk thru bankflood bazarre looking for the lost frost game saga, the bang gambit.

Shit & sink: should the city try to stop the hog from setting up slop?

For where is words dares evermore dirt.

RAKED SCREEN

A HITCH, a stick,
succession of circumscision in the pits, a single twiggy bough becomes the boggle, wooden token taken & shaken, branded the number of a hewer & sewered thru fibrous plaster… it's sticking… inkwhips…

shut off your listings! Your screen is overcollecting… & repeating!

… meddling whelps, taps at the old door, tightning wraps,
dead propellors churn burnwater, caked mud turns on a lathe, latent transformers go stick, go stark, go staring, go naked, go wicking, wailing, biting, raving…

Too much! Let it bleed! It's stuff we don't need – let it wash!

The General's bursts ringing in his ears, Zeen sits muddily at the rampart as the little rivers run backwords, disparaging the wrongly rolling waste:

You wretch! You rag! You rabbling baggage! Worthless fragment, forgotten scrap! Forget your wretched caper – The robes of majesty are but the rags of infirmity!

He rubs his own rags on stone & casts his letters into the current before jumping in himself, to be raked into pieces & eaten by mudworms...
   & see up close what things his screens have captured...

PILE OF GODS

CUT heads jut just above screen a half mile down, wedged in cramped cages in caves, killed or saved. This is legend, as it happens.
   A slab rocks into balls & balls sliding down a ply, flying metal chips stick to steel stacks making radio contact, protein portions catch on points of iron, chewed as chosen sources of metamorphic biscuit.
   And we, I, it, this mobile ark-encumbered work-crew (yes, it is us! onsite, with job) drill a tiny tunnel into the layers, umbrellas to catch pebbles & keep watch for lost godheads,
   upsidedown underground cherrypicker reaches thru fenced strata, quaking curtains.
   Collapsed cobbles trigger boulders breaking & ambushed onlookers spend the rest of their blinking days in extended rituals of self-blinding, rolling up the rim—
   Sorry, try again.
   Legible tablets tossed down a mineshaft, explosive snaps of lettereaters' earthjaws, ends of ledges snap like crackers, rumble of enlargening hunger, swish & enormous suction of gutted rockswallows,
   rancid water drips thru the rocks, thirst of our captured flower,
   as condom-encapsulated microphones slip thru narrow holes to feed our frantic exhibition.

I, I, it, it, we, this, it can't tell when we got wrenched into such a trap, into such a trap we got wrenched I can't tell when.

Rolling up these balls of paper,
a new fuss for sissyfoots short on daily wage -
is this the math of our new myth?

The new youth become legends by leaping off ledges & diving across the chasm & landing in the pool, or dry dying in the gutter.

cold & cramped after initial collapse, bodies lost, heads collected.

But firy need ignites our insides, electric brains burst legless thru the doors covered in mud & slime & sink onto preverbial knees crying: *I'm alive.*

A surgical glove tugs our ankles with electric tape & six feet of cable, of unknown intention & arousing superspicion –

They're always showing us things.

They sniffed my fingers right off & dipped them in egg for the baking... my eyes...

& this just one of many channels in this latest occupational nightmare. The rest are rotten also.

FRICTION HORSE I

WATERWORN, waterborn of riverbeds, dead seas & deserts, these tossing machines, the dogs of sleep that dwell in concrete folds,

it, it, I, I, us, they cannot bear to hear the monolithic bigengine sands scratch the brick of their sinking saucepan pier.

Flaking upon the pain of expulsion they wither & discover an alternate purity in the blacklettered flats of plastic chamber after little bits drift in swift liquid drain, & the bigger chunks sifted with microsoft screens.

Mouths flap at the outfall: *every handful of tax is grit in the gears of the wealth tractor, impairing, disrepairing powers in peril of barrels of prowess,*
it cracks
our teeth.
Can acid application dissolve our chaff?

Our beds are cursed by course cleavage dripping south over our feed, swimming in mormud where thick mor bobs upon compiling dead-ponds
as course oatmeal pours, flows of branchaff, milldust, unground oat-husk, whole greets boil till burst, cracked fragments mixed with oil, the blood of broken engines.

Uncautious thru rising fog, lashless thru strewn elephant sands, the red eye unwinking passes phantasmic fabric of fastdissolving drum tossing in this thunderous wash.

Unnatural habitat.

SAND EXTRACTED FROM GRITCHAMBER

FIERCE pieces pierce loose planks, roll back grit with a hint of a flack.

Preset tents: a bad place to past out in.

I, it, we get the cuts in our necks, index, appendix, infected guts, we gut to tag the load of lead cargo thick with knots, knock against pits, not the net of steel cake, the little shitbulls, teeth stick out boxes.

Gunked liquid licks us hard with beak to back kickoff scabs, sparks a bokko blitz in our pinched liquors.

Golphers gang up, fling clubs at a puzzle over open cracks.

Royal flash steeps a pack of birdkill, ignites the toxic match.

King Adam cancells gates, letting extra current sting the bulging lake nameless.

Another tax break attack? Fuck that.

Grinding his soaken talkmouth back into the downflow past, Zeen squated in his customized tinkertanking sandsink & thatted out a huge volume of fresh sand.

How to consume the ever increasing supply?

He washed off his overbitten lipped modelnozzle & gave it a whirl.

Steam irrupted from his least clogged pores & squeezed out a thick track of fake crude, the black goo of unrefined message mudmath.

Precontaminated, unfit for the clean motors of oversedimented bank, the toxic stew flew cracking & babbling into its deepcut tailing sink, which sucked it in with magnetically magnified thirst.

Hundreds of black barrels buckled at the unforecast feast with excited little tubes rattling under the chlorescent lamplight.

Dozens of buckling barrels black out at the rattling fork-edges of tubular feast to later awaken in an unstifled sneeze of fluorescence.

FRICTION HORSE II

GOLD mass dipped in molten glass is the core in this empty vessel is also hallow as a fissure in a hoof & filled to the roof with this, our heated friction horse, our exacting thunderhearse, an unrehearsed roughrubbing beast to weld pieces in the whirlwind flux, a horse with one dusty hoof stirring slag in dunebusting vortices,

a fond-of-found-food function-horse that eats its way thru tubular conveyance, layers of eruption sprung from flood, thru seven muddy courses of bunker with sharpened lip & sugarlicking hungertongue.

It slurps thirsty at the bottom rung, bloated tummy rubbing rough riffs of coral rock smooth & scratching the flawless surface with frantic furrows. Its existence depends upon the presence of resistance.

Like I remember one summer before the horses escaped metallic runs were poured at the ingate & a sad ball of silver sand landed in the riser of mould rendering us happy because our castle was already sinking & sliding as a glacier receding & I noticed its tower become a slumping pinnacle & took it upon myself to rub it with my scoop & it loosened & leaned & the whole thing shook & so did you because we could finally see as sure as day the wet spots thru which the muddy waters ooze & in letting the slender colourstreams fall from hand over foam banks & guiding it & letting it glide & ooh those designs it left behind!

That was the summer of sand.

& the brown smoke that rises over dead rivers smothers your upcurl spouts of pink magic like lightning fuses its tubes for passage & so we corrugated our metal beds because we love the look of that floss smeared brown.

But the stone age always begins with a ferment, & a square tank stone-stripped in the cross-section lying in shallow clay-loam depressions sheds its sorted pebbles in the freeze-thaw mania of popcycling chimney, like remember when... *Zeen you miserable twit!*

The General.

This is exactly what we didn't want – Overflows! What is the preferred method of release? Tanks for the memories or banks? I insist upon a bypass.

GRIT ABSTRACTED FROM SANDTRAP

COLD scores crawl lax up & back ship's crunkling stomachs, seasoned crabwalkers chuck acrid anchor deep in rancid bank backward.

Sick critters on twobanks batt hunks of debris back & back across the cresting water.

Vents & stacks of underwater tractors swim past, unprotected from flocking wreckage.

Dozens gather at banks to salvage scraps, but the cruel arms of cemented sediment snap back, committing casual massacre with the care of a king.

Down at the minute-biting riverteeth a hiking battalion of decapitated bodies stumble thinkless into an ancient exstream, poking fresh out of the evershifting fixtures.

Profuse headlines.

FRICTION HORSE III

OLD Operator Zool stands rubbergloved in the decomposing canal, a massive stone surgeon inside the morbid concretion of rotting skinwalls,

a hot rod dipped in sick bladder, he hooks the stone with a pair of tongs used for lifting mammoth blocks from reverse-sloped valleybottoms, fills his drawers & asks for more.

Blind, cold, deaf, dead, dumb, fettered with gouts & tormented with stones, he spurns the bleeding at its banks & works its diggings with a flat slab, a tablet for grinding the impress out of every splashing facet.

> Bone poor & skin rich, it lives
> inside a drum, stretched,
> petrified in cursed crust, a wooden sleeper
> in its pulpy core, wrapped
> in the inner tissues of succulent flesh,
> an erosive worm with a tooth for its own cocoon
> fakes its cuts & marks its base boundary
> between the 'A' & 'C' horizons,
> a broken stone of silence, enlivened
> by a bolt...

PEBBLES SUBTRACTED
FROM DIGESTIVE TRACT

THE VOLUME doublifies itself every seven years.

Then how to contend with such exsescent overdoublage?

Zeen could feel the teeth of the General gnawing at his hipwaders.

He gazed upriver & gasped, letting his manual message billow out of his widest fleshmouth with amplitudinal enhancement:
I call for a moratorium!
In response, the ongoing flood becomes evenmore awash with producers' reports,
  the river flowing thick with great wads of waterlogged paperpulp like
  a trickle of soup endensened with salted crackers, all selfimportantly muttering the same suburgent word:

bludderrubberwetterspitterripperupperguttermuterover-floweruntertowerwhetherbedderbidderfitterfatter

Zeen coughed up a few more pebbles & a pair of petrified paperballs &
  planned several more expansions of his massive mothball reservoir.

RISEN SEDIMENT SKIMMED

THE PLASTICK power of flesh corrupts a rough election compressed
  as every arteryfisher knows his knots must loose their greasy humors
    when wick'd thirst-fires melt him fretting, chafing in his own
      crammed capons & pea-hens, chickens in the shit
        sitting, swimming in pools of it. Hot carpets, hot horses, hot skins beat together, a-glister with charcoal, morbid secretion

for the ones they smothered & made mountains of, each loaf packed, wrapped in plastic, bird-proof, worm-proof, proof of interrenal ejection –

Heureaka! necks crack beneath magnetic hands glovely gliding the quick wheel

as plastic clay vigors up bandcrashing caterpillars, waxing up trouble in a mothless pit of promotion,

each growing lump brings to bear the movement of its chisel, frozen shells & growing stones, expanding fashions of plastic power,

extruding combs over cosmetic boxes, resin crammed into moulds, instantly cool...

But trash clothing, sludge settles for less so the effluent can keep moving

dirtless, putty-like, explosive of purget like bicycle-pumps firing off at the stroke of a lever,

knife-holes cut in doughy slabs of unpalatable blast-muck masquerading as honeybuns,

mines of limitless dynamite & other sources

of light, a frame made of steel tube, pissproof roof of rubbercoated nylon,

elastic-panted hordes of soggy children with untidy luggage cut quick-frozen meat under supermarket chains,

lumps of undertabletop process cheddar, radio rod of chicken wire...

Even a neat, plastic-covered plunge is not exact enough for a dead man's veranda. But enough of that & more of this,

the dregs are needing. Every water should be cast upon its basin's feces so that the bottom powder residents enfiercen the fermentation,

a pestilent contagion, the impressions which the bile make upon this villous coat, to mark it -
mechanical scrapers drive the collected into a hopper at the tankbase, shit
sinks & soap swims, passes
pumped thru pools. Live
inside of it.

JETSAM SNAGGED ON MAGYPNOTIC SKYHOOKS

PURTURBED in gravity, the mammoth powersource releases another load...
& the infamous old loon finally cracks, turning 90 in a heap of trash & robust gas.
A forgotten boulderbag of cuts loosens its flagging fortunes, & then the inevitable shreddings & other forgettable tragedies,
castaways that die with unsliced anonymity, unspent cash scattered into undiscovered oceans, fragments left to tinker fruitlessly in a pregrammatical void,
ephemeral watertitans spread their weak limbs in attempt to gather all they can...
Mixmaster Zeen's hyperoptic lures such glass giants by their short fibres into his cheaper streams, pulls their gravitationous cores over by the cold plugs of their own fields, entrappted in his hydrotoxic circuitry.
His divining turbines give off a ruffled atmospheric byproduct that rubs the flesh like the static skin of a freshly ripened ionic peach ready to step down from its home tree.

Even CEO Attackfish say they would rather expand their own rooftop realms but are driven into Zeen's charged fields by the premise of unlimited hydroelectoral gravy, hot manna from magypnotic heaven.

The demand for the fruit of this rumour creates a false boom amongst the more irregulated labs in the lower windspheres, where jars of whispering specimen are breezily processed.

But once inside the folds of Zeen's tinking sandtank, once swimming in soft waters between the pink banks of his overcharged waterbeds, they find the electrocratic nugget dangerously beefed with poisonous millomites.

With their very bloodlines strapped to the hooks of Zeen's gypnotic trap, these fish of modern enterprise have no choice but to muzzle the freemouths of their own production, lest they accidently injest his deadly bolt.

The accelerated dischords of Zeen's manufictional powersander blow a filtered broadcast of graded nightmare all across the gridded basin, a refined stream of renegade voltage designed to blow apart any hope of divertification.

Even us, it, I, I, this mobile ark-engine, our own new substation, designed to run underground distribution lines illicitly spliced into the mainlines of power to feed domestic amplifiers with a custom zirconium seed, has been crudely ripped from its subterranean base & rerouted into the menacing swish of Zeen's widening currents, its urgent message swept from managed earthlips & pushed thru his helectropic anus.

Miles & miles of lines of electoral voltage lie in immense tangles at the quivering stations, in desperate need of upgrade.

But the road to death is paved with the graves of the living, & such a blight of scathing filtration requires the bite of microbial acid fantasy, the kind of sky-tech solution only Zeen's electro-shock-revived cementary plunder can provide -

older stones quarantined & mashed into magnetic gravel for new hotroads, fresher tablets scratched out & stuck deep into the immencing banks to reinforce the paleomagnetic pillars of regimented bedrock enhancements.

Dire straits! Under gears & gallows & frozen irons, chained to darkness under an inky plume of prophesy smeared on the roofs of forbidden channel, the old loon abandons its queendom & flies south as sumppits pump off unwanted floodstuff, fording the chronic waste-river at its bank of greatest shortage with suicidal invest & insurgent intention.

Terrorforces of mastered nature stratify thru their fullest laminar tributaries, ready to bag the lamming loon & wipe its fragile wings right off the counterfeit map.

The clean sweep of operation render-under-seizure nets a whopping catch of corrupted chemical, disturbed current, perverted sediment nabbed from swelling banks & a young AC radio inadvertently suckling loose energy from the gargantuan mammoth of current.

Forgivable under the allprovoking stress of riverrage? Zeen's top apprentice, Enid the Omeban Watereater, thinks not & proposes a second sweep: *if every fugative appliance rips off our currents then all juice in the end will be consumed in pilferationist orgy.*

Mere ideology! snorted Zeen & he seized both the Omeban & the detained radio, wrung both dry of juice & delivered their shrivelled remains to his nearest generator.

Such cruelty! Such pitiless rage! But even these ephemeral flowers, once in the vortex of Zeen's torrential imachinations, lose their outer petals & wither back into earlier carnations, one becoming valuable crude & the other flailing backward into an inverted pit of senselessness.

Meanwhile, the old loon perks up at the arial bordercrossing, having nearly envaded the massive pull of Zeen's field, then encounters a final horrific smear of wingsnapping stratospheric turbulence & falls headfirst into the blackened pool.

THE PROTOZOANS

VERTICAL HATCH

TWITCHING fibrils of light burn into muscular biomass quivering,
  electric branches snap & crack under hail of sky-eggs, rain of charged protoplasm, auricular break-out, lightshow, life-shock -
  athwart the forking vectors of vertical influence, this, it, I, I, us, this contagious crew shakes Zeen's baking battery & cracks
  open his starving capacitors & gethers to gather another glut of infrastructure, wires, poles, converters & transformers to mix & splice with raw matter, nasal passage & a megametamorphomagknotic matwarp for a plan & hang from throbbing drafts & erect from the jerking rockbed a pulsing grid acriss & across a sinking basin.
  Freshly hatched protozoans crawl back thru charged petraplasmic rivers, sharp olfactory nozzles bursting out in dense odiferous matrix, limbs unformed, nostril blasts unstifled, mouths wide open, bodies soft, vulnerable to snatching.

DROWNED ODD

BEATEN UNEVEN with bean-size hail, even beaten with high-pressure spray under manifold mass of small-bottle retail, we all fall under & the pumping of mammoth trunks is done at the cost of the hoses' exhaustion.
  & this stripped out flatfield is chop full, loaded, overflow with the debris of such things. All on us
  it's dumped: boards & nails, twisted metal sheets shot from windwhirl
  gouging hard ground, radioactive horse trailer tossing, four freed in clouds of hay & trash
  under the rain of frozen peas, he looked into the pasture & saw the dirt devil expand, glowing toxic orange, bags flapping rapid
  & a rabid iron cat breaking yellow from crumpling barn, swallowed & tossed
  shrieking into the steeltongued mouth of an overturned auger, machine shop doors ripped from hinges, hurled slashing, scratching new ruts in noxious hayfields, tractors mangled, barbecues strewn, burnt & bent & mingling across a craterscape of make-shift pits... ripped-open vacuum-bags hang from trees, somethings freed...
  & our asphalt roofs were pummelled, drummed, bedroom window inching open, our stuff, our clothes, it blew
  in swirls... & with trunks & hoses we battled the raging thrash,

big machine punching mud over the ranking load to smother... black smoke blown into mouths & nostrils, hovers over beating hearts...

Images captured in ancient books, on digital camera, the streaming download, our roofs & rubberheads, coats & tents

on & on were pummelled & drummed.

ANXIETY OF INFLUENCE

SHAKEN & hazed, the fraudulent Engineer crouches in his fake lab & keeps an anxious eye upon his many watches,

watches panels, pipes & wires for signs of the next event to overtax his drains,

watches meters & gauges for excessive discharge, his instruments for undo influence,

shivers at the notion of combination, the fearful interconnections, the introduction of the unwanted...

& is it true? the ancient rumour that the streams are merging...

Don't be stupid! You know as well as I the two rivers, one pure & the other putrid, were combined at the dawn of the day of the ocean's recession, at the very conception of their confluent construction. All that remains is to separate them.

Fighting his own snooze he studies his samples between the nod & snap cycles, his ancient samples embalmed in a glass ball, the solution to future

pollution. Dilution? Or diversion?

A glare, a gleam, vivid camera reflection, an icy spheric beaming its mark upon delicate readings. A lash,

it blinks

again, a reflect! That damned eye.
Zeen grabs the offending occulant from its pert entuskment & tosses it into his maxiflow toilet & even as he ponders his precious instruments, his pipes, their eventual outfall & design flaws,
he flushes it down,
sees the sharp-focused pupil toss clockwise counting down his gurgling drain.
Let THAT be my eye in the system! he shrieks & tears his panel to pieces.

ASSINIBOIAN EATING ZOO

STEWING BACK in his machinations, Zeen sits chewing his meal-brick in a pool of chosen fuel, pondering the exit-hoses that conjure the extended ritual of rebirth & the dilemma of how to sip soda without straw.
Rising, he wanders his dry dreambeds, dropping metallic crane-seeds down virtual boreholes.
His thinking runs double down his corduroy rivets, trippling down his bulging tributaries.
Is it any wonder that according to prophecy the prophet's snake swallows the king's?
or that the river of lower tonnage forgoes its name at the forks & runs red with mud, the blood of a billion zoans,
identity swallowed by its superior, as if unchanged for this generous redoubling of its matter? as if the one swallowed the other rather than the both eating the each & the other & names be damned – who will choose the downstream colour?
& how would a real engineer treat such a combined influence?

Such were the questions that flowed & choked thru Zeen's exploding channels in the afterbath of his primary manipulations.

Excess growth, excess food, everything in abundance & the channels are plugged.

Impatient, he tickles a hose or two toward the legitimate ends of his existence.

The machine jolts & gasps a tiny cloud of semi-digested particulate.

Mildly shocked, Zeen rushes onto the scene of his recreation with modified heardrums, nozzle & goggle, the current equipment for long-range perception & dashes upon a new theory of amortality.

& with a gush of false gusto he opens his facets & launches his next mission, a zoo where guests are asked to eat the animals,

& are at last required to.

GOLGONOOZAN SNOOP

LIKE razor-sharp death-screeches of mammals strapped to an electric bank is the call of the bagged zoans dragged across a horrific dawn...

Rubberbooted with longtooth amber umbrella wideopen Zeen enters the flooding city & assumes it is Golgonooza, not knowing the nameplate at its gates had been taken

from elsewhere to lure tourists. Volvox is its real name & no we don't know what it means.

Oblivious to such anonymfamy but aware of the invinsibility of his prey, Zeen soon also dons his Loon-goggle & Bloomnozzle to better sense in the mist of beastly blooms.

& the zoans begin to appear, much smaller than he had envisioned, but much larger than himself & menacing grewsome even thru his gogular enhancements.

Mindful of turbulent sludge, with gourmet zoogleal meal-mix he aims to lure the four, one of the each of the one, north into his improvizing utopic construction, where nuth's affront & locks unlip & fonts flow froth like sky-green gob goes gray goes math goes mosh,

or take them by force, capture all the expert eaters & imprison them in his secondary reactors, doomed to live out their days ecstatic in the paradisiacal stratum of his habitat, eating his curse & waste.

Now he drags the four backwards thru sunless rivers, reversing their trail & hiding his predatorial plunder back in his pool of impenetrable darkness,

blocks their cries with wads of guaze...

& the sky snake, waking, blinks...

& Zeen flees, breaking iron chains, lets fall the great rockslab blocking the entrance to his cavernous lab

& the foiled portcullis slides back in its groove.

Thrice the tempest presses the tapering needle of flint around the rocky pinnacle as vultures circle

& a crack of thunder rings the wide sky, rivers run backward & banks jump back & slump

& all at once the Sun beams inthru cracks in Zeen's dark cavern revealing his secrets

& the tempest showers the lab with toxic debris as thick black smoke chokes out from ailing machines.

ZOOGLEAL MASS MATRIX

fast & loose to bind the pondering slabs,
  they burp, bubble & crack electric, the beds, they breath & sneeze & speak & spit, alive
  with limestone, gravel, coal & plastic. In the sick haze of stuck twilight mats
  are deepened & ripened to compel hungry zoans further into this rich substrata, kingmeals
  for sewerserfs, crude allures for raw recruits without rule or notion of hope, out-of-work-horses without a ratrace to run in:
  Zilyad Arrowfoil the mannypaddled swimmer spinning angry vortices in the eutrophic excitement of his saturated vicinities,
  Flajella Mastigon with her many plasmodic whips, holding her latest host hostage for the hunger of her invaginated anterior gullet,
  even Enid the Omeban Watereater, fresh from her latest pilferationist orgy, is resurrected, yanked up lip first into this yellowjellied paradise,
  where thick liquor spills thru spinning arms, perforated nozzles splaying
  from axial pivot, trickles thru juicy substrata, collected in drains & stonelayers over underdrains as windsprays soak the hot air. THUS
  INVITED, the zoans will live a media-rich existence in the filth
  & shine of zoogleal film, a gelatinous mass of growing organic matter made
  of bodies embedded in the tight cracks of confluencial matrix of swollen capsules, snakeskin film
  sloughed off by the shear force of flow...

THE PILOT

ENDRENCHED in black goo, the spent loon twice encircles the red-hot spot & collapses.
 Feebly it pecks at the dot & lets up a long, low call as mattressed tunnel of red air narrows
 to a funnel, tubes poke thru the thin membrane of a tiny I-pod, little film of yogurt trickling down thru deeper scratches,
 burning to gravy & tripping a chicken dinner to lull a trapped alarm clock to sleep between hard rock splinters, tripped a fan to stir a turning turkey...
 in livid moments of brightness
 every leak becomes manifest.
 The underground Sun runs its gold-soaked rainbows round our shrunken temples & thru our frozen ears, drilling deep into the book of thrills.
 Entombed inside the ancient beating beacon house of holy rhythm in every animate machine is a tiny pilot with electric fingers that pluck the visceral circuits with titanian keys & squeeze the shower of charge from the zirconian flower.
 What could awaken that immaculate corpse?
 To evade the underqualified Engineer's magypnotic discorporate eye, we, we, I, I, this ark-engine crew, it prepares our ten drills in the thickest thatch of night & bores our guide-holes thru sheets of black ice from the safety of steel cages,

protection from thawing sharks, killer whales, watersnakes & other sharp-toothed zoa of the underriver arena, this inland ocean of extinction.

Nearer our target & the aromatic tang of ancient flavours flowers about us, ripping into our private cages, waking our prize elephants.

Inside the guide-hole, we drill the tunnel just under the escapist's cellular capsule, the final crust to be chipped away with handtools.

But how, how to break thru to this delicate cavity, this trembling veil of cocoon where the treasure is trapped?

Closer, we inch, the dirt, we itch, the dust, the shaking rocks, this incessant agitation, aggravate vibration deeper perturbs the inner portions with the risk of rupture or torture to trigger the rockfall that will kill our quest in earth-breaking quake.

Who is that sleeper dreaming deep within the inner chamber?

Who have we been feeding all these weeks thru this cheap yellow esophagus & hearing breath with this tiny electric ear?

What offspring of primordial sewer will come on our mammalian elevator to greet the throng above? Should we desire to meet it?

Will it walk on its own? Or will we carry it, carry it, carry it? & what to tell if we find the body dead in its cell?

But we don't

find it at all, only a soaking mess where its fragile bleeding body had slept.

The colours of the chamber gleam, the aromatic flavours soar, but the source itself was drained & dragged away. Video evidence shows a tiny amortal creator with a hammer & tongs & a tank full of gas. He made off with the pilot & left this message.

In icy afterbath, in utterly spontaneous cold rain, the Sun Ship ascends...

& the fallen loon's mourning song echoes across the hollow drill hall.

ORANGE TOXIC

HOT air, dry beds, hot hot flash.

The four power-sucking protazoans, newly arrived & desperate for feed, push power supply to the upmost limit of Zeen's resources.

They arrived at the zoo with little notion of status as workers or guests or inmates or meals for all three, later to discover Zeen's intention to dissolve all such distinctions in an ionic acidbath of alternating current.

In the devastation dawn he exercises his anxious missiles, then snoozes under traffic-beams as his critical staff dump rancour & ruckus into the backbench of his nap.

Reaping the harvest of current invisibility, a traveling bouyant eight-ball reverses its path with blooming sales & hidden outboard motor,

diving under, averting the eyes of buzzard-guided stream-cyclists,

web-surfers fitted with engine & tiller, state-of-the-art riverskaters,

ravenous wingless vultures riding makeshift rafts, hard-core canoe-heads masquerading as cabin-cruisers.

Wet with its latest lickings, the machinery of modern tornado scrawls its gratuitous graffiti upon the barns of modern justice,

sour grapes twisting in vine-wrapped walls pierce the freshest juice-clouds, bursting the ancient skins of celestial bladder.

The river runs toxic orange with swirls of green & a faint blue sheen,

criminal crash pilot task force to invade the bioelectric pages of tomorrow's Sun with miniature horse charms strapped to backs burned in the earth-core,

a 200 pound stack of newspaper stuck in a high gravity rut without a reader,

rejected letters fall free, recombine & attach parasitic to the first available host

thru scraped heal, cut ankle, shotgun-pattern back perforations, excess earth inhalation,

& worms grow big, hang from trees, dangle from treads stretching, glowing, drenched in pulp of juice of orange, of, of...

Zeen wakes with a snap & roars. *The stockrapers plan to rake hides across the bulk flow to stem my accidental upgrade!*

Angry urges rip electric thru his raw muscles. Pouring another cup of tonic, he allows his voicebox to creak out one lost message: *the channels of massive spillage need to be redeemed in momentous measure. Let leak what must be leaked! Dam what must be dammed!*

Like the critical cankerworm a mothering moth reverts in its larval moment, the invasion proceeds in reversing stages of ripeness.

FULLESOPHAGAL BLOCKAGE

TO FEED to death! This is the stuff of overtaxiderby most immaculate! Who stuffed the golden goose?
 In the world of amortal mechanics, shortage & excess are but the gist of balance,
 black & red data in the crude calculus of heat-production & tissue-formation, irksome to accountancy, nuisance to smooth-running war.
 Everything the mind can drink is woven into this 20,000 mile supply line, stretching trail of meal, the elongated chain of linkprocessors, packers, hauliers & intermediate eaters, the well-trodden path now broken – at a single link!
 The foodmiles are blocked.

CHAIN FEAST

LOCOMOTION is slow...
 customary plasmic protrusions extrude from his huge Winnibeggo -
 often he lies suspended for many compressed underriver hours, trapping food on his stretching & shrinking axepods,
 or slowly rolls along a moving bed strapped to a drafty substratum in Zeen's reactor, obsessivley assembling & dissembling his microtubular core thru inert media, converting youthfull biomass into ageless protoplasm, hooking them onto his infernal growth system, strictly addictive,
 Omeba Aenidocrass, a.k.a. Enid the Watereater, a full professor in the art of digestion before her untimely

demise, left behind a hidden legacy of unfinished dinners,

& herself an unfinished dinner, engaged rapturous in the holy role of host to any number of parasitic guests & willingly served as prey to many a remorseless predator.

Dissatisfied at the peak of the heap, Enid liked to stake out a place at the base & maintained a well-fed suspicion toward the existence of such a perilous perch as the top of a chain.

She loved to be devoured, food for fishes, drowned for powder, buried for epicurean worm festivals & partially resurrected.

Enamoured in her own luminescent stigma, she would show you her holes & boast about what it's like

to eat & be eaten, as in a media biofilm chainfeast where bacteria feed protozoans feed worms feed birds feed the ornithologizer's hungry goggle.

Face smeared with skin-food, Enid would in the same day gun down big game & skim the microbial jungle with membranous suckmouth while donating an organ or a limb to her carnivorous competitors & later insist upon being buried alive long enough to offer up vast portions of her own flesh further downstream in the everlasting fester.

& it is this double purpose which made her perfect to labour in Zeen's secondary processors.

EXPANDING BURIAL SUBPLOT

BONE pounded down to powder to make the urn that mimics a rare morphology, ornamental neck & shoulders, elbows, bands & panels, the four vases' bottoms poked with fine punctures, internal rim deeply bevelled...

her food-vessel skeleton burials required a coarse pottery absorbed in secondary protolithic tradition,

Enid was a unique creature.

But now the feed is building without an expert eater. Now the pits are filled with powder, rivers choked in sugary wads of freshly fallen electric manna.

The world vegetation network becomes overloaded, nutritionally overdosaged,

the power of plants to choose by root the mineral part of their fuel

is lost.

PURGATORIAL RESIDENCY

A PERMANENT state of detergency!

Cleansing, purging, an antiseptic swimulation in various ulcerated conditions of motormoutherant fantasy.

Miscible synthesis, exquisite liquid concoction, soluble solids, dirt-like solution.

Chop, chop. Soap hamburger, *chomp*.

Gently deterred, the terminal gentry swarms around bony deathpiles, sniffing for sweetness & finding only the broken portions

of a lost potion, stick a fork in it...

& their lotion is lungeless in suspension, fingers of sun smudge the unbudgable substance, soap & salt & fat & oil & all in lubrication launchpad bonanza burn, flesh grows lax & spongy, with urgency, with hot air, linttrap, spincycle of power required for a dryer.

The word arrives of possible divine detergency, a rapid Zapponification adding undulating allowances upon axidentical inhibition, galgolbizonovulvinade the active agent of adsorption that forms the familiar useless foam, exquisite scum in hardwater letting spread & penetrating fully over & thru a filthy zero utility article such as this.

Fade to freezing integer...

Zoonspor Epicomplexica, masterlaunderer, shivers in her cage. A severed link, she hears the processors running wrong, chains whipping off their runners, cycles shorting.

Once in charge of synthetic beginnings, she fears being cut off entire & starving at the fringes.

Before being lured into Zeen's purgatorial bioreactors, she was the final mouth on a custom processor, an electric appliance for cleaning, mixing, chopping, shredding & otherwise poofing otherways unpalatable food for ritual consuming, doing all with her errorproof inner computer & with only the tiny technical spoof that none but herself could run it for all of its excess customization.

A born parasite incapable of solo motion, Zoonspor was the first to be lured into the engineered transport currents

& the last to leave.

VEHICULAR CONFLUENCE

BOLD OR brash, bluff headland, a mass of borrowed rubble rubbed along a line of shore unsettled. Figures of vertical prominence carved
  in stone relief, sheer descant of cliffface, this refuse of typeface. Massive breach
  of bank, arsonary icebrush combs thru ashes, mountains funneled under gallery pressure. Post-traumatic rumours
  tip off of lavish purchase. Cuffed confluence, disordered enormity. The grim-faced members
  seek overnight answers, shackled in the evacuated drawers of withdrawal. These are the spots where banked-up ranks
  of motorcycle metal are overturned by UV shovel & pent-up seizures
  are pinned-up flat for better reception. The sobbing waters crest heavy
  with buoyant beer-trucks encrusted & bomb-ridden minibus & 10 more
  immobile homes engulfed. Tough cutting tigerprobe tucked in
  to track backwoods washing in the backstreets, now banned. A power-hungry
  pooch lowers its flag & raises its leg over solitary cosmetic ticket. Under
  the floodwater stresses we'll piss on whatever we can get. The pesticidal
  credit-diggers extend a branch & go guttergreen in a well-ditched sewer tribute.

Mouth open wide breathing smashed bits of dike, higher & higher enhanced wave action
 collapses the embattled sandbag expansion into Saturday gulfed up to a higher
 shore, golfed up to a higher score, rancid rain & septic snow, toxic hail
 & electric forks lashed.

Much smaller than he had envisioned, but much larger than himself & menacing grewsome even thru his gogular enhancements.

SCHMUTZDECK

 bloodlines strapped to the hooks of gynoptic trap, shot along refined streams
 of renegade voltage, Flajella Mastigon clutches her anxious whips & flings
 her manyappendaged bulk fullways over the flushing polyvynal falls & falls

out of the guts of her giganto-termitic host & flat upon the sandy bed

of Zeen's pandaemonious schmutzdeck, crowded, heavy, slow sand,

thick clot, thick cloud, sick waterfall muddled, obscured, erased, disturbed,

confused with influence, the thick of the action! BACK IN the saddle, body

rolls in slow spiral perpendicular to the path of locomotion & beats backward,

vibrating tip, gullet & rods at the anterior end, drawn towards the dim light she swims

ecstatic amidst the rocks, snapping whips for speed & steering, a biomass

star on suspended film, shooting thru a fractal galaxy of gravel, at home

in turbidity, in bright green joy, at one with cholorplastic massexodus from cytoplasm

to black coffee turmoil, at home in the baking chaos of Zeen's bioreactors,

she built her house right into the rough rockbed, substrata, brownshell, spiny collar

around the opening, lines of power spliced in & connected to her many sockets.

Doubting the strength of the structure, Zeen attempted to smash

its walls with a colossal magnetic needle & the rigid matter cracked

into fragments that instantly reassembled tighter & stronger & coated in slime

& covered in moss, as fixed growth in crushed rock, an ideal site

for Flajella's daily binge of strong drink sprinkled from Zeen's rotary arms. She grows,
  her slime thickens & is at last sloughed off as a new layer begins
  to build as spent matter is collected in underdrains & sent
  to the pumphouse where she waits, fixing her illicit connections,

INK RAINS

THE RUSH of oil from roaring fans
  shifts with the breath of scraping jets. Helicopters crash in cymballic gaseous concoction. A plethora of sky-wrecks rain upon the desert, in the settling sands the rash of debris forming an intricate epic of graffiti. Warming up
  the rockets in his sky-high hottub, Zeen catches the wind of destructive rhythm & to its gravelly tune concocts the text for his newest tattooing. Thus he rubs his palms & begins
  the rhythmic waterslapping that will send his dusty summons out into the night to awaken the hordes of slumbering soldiers & sailors that extend
  his repetitious bugling. Black ink rains upon the pulpfields, crumbling rock pours into this bituminous tar to form the paste that is later pressed into the soil of pulp to make the roads thru which our arms can make their rolling way. This is how
  it all begins. Solid, asphaltic, septic, electric, the city pours itself out in monthly overruns & the rapid re-

versing currents push in to damn their dissolution. The bailers
  bail, the jailers jail & the everyready culprit has a concrete pulpit for pissing from. Beyond the order of cosmic concrete necessity timeframes expand, past
  the power of regional tower, Zeen's machines churn the current with bloated budget & extrapolated stratagem, strip the fallout beyond the call of municipal dollar.
Borrowing up & running loose with the luck of the dikes, Zeen explains his excessive flooding thus:

> *What choices have we? Whether its water or roads or bridges or batteries or plants or dams or pumps or refineries, everything's more expandable than it is expendable. How can we play clean & safe without the everpresent threat of mortal danger?*

We, I, it, this toxic convey of sewerserfs, have come to expect his rejected recommendations to be later tabled & accepted & sent back to us, modified with mechanical parts & floated downriver.

  Our mouths grow wider & wider to enable us to swallow whatever shit he sends us. We build our dikes out of the rubble that washes down the pike while our waterfront properties are constantly washing away.

  All of our music is polluted with this ragged rhythm. All of our dances are stuck in this jagged chasm.

  Flood protection? Weekly we declare a state of emergency & our bridges become the matter for his wrath to build its bouldered dams. *We'll blow up that bridge when we come to it*, he says.

BLUERED BUILDUP

SOLIDARITY cracks the expansive crossroads with quarter-point cuts
 & the devil's lake empties into its permanent diversion – we'll all swallow all we're able.
 Jet lag, red lake, lag in the jet lake, cash grab, crashcab, the floodgates of bloodbanks
 rise & fall in fits of sedimented laughter & even the Sun submits to the revolting scratch of photoradar.
 The full flow of floodmoney buries the burning ends of summer, ultraviolet barriers & ozone oceans open slow as we lapse at length into permanent laughtrack.
 Open that trap & gaze upon the skin of the milk of official urge turning.
 Ink runs west released to transplant dogs sniffing, well-dressed ghosts wasted on sewage, headless corpses hunt for cash in the churn of blue shadow, blasts harassing happy campers & school bombs hit road family hard in vacation comedy burial subplot.
 All things filtered, some extra charges dropped in for a taste of future hazard forkcast.
 Overkill? Yeah, a little more never burns what was there before unless the mudmath of current horizon runs riot over wrathful rate hikes raking across our lifebanks.
 But the shear pain of certainty exhilarates the ever-tightening cycles of scrap we wield in.
 At last the lonely loon sits spinning its tale of woe from beyond the roof of current inflation, where growth outgrows its parasitic paradise & succumbs to outright cannibalistic play, plagues of fresh litigation

colonies sprouting daily, teething as attacktalks, nesting in the softer patches of urban desert.

Expensive? Not if you think like this: the press of lumber's knotted deadlines produces the terms of gain undercutting your framework with a produce-cycle that incubates a harsh fiduciary include effectively capping the border-market keyport cutshare. So there.

Death grows & dies & so does life. It's all juice residue running in circular worktubes.

On the one hand is another hand & even that's but another fast leaking lifedrain, fragile beast of time.

BIONIC BLOOPER

BLUE pull, blue plot, fast red boost...

red race, red rows, raw red moon, the blue prints bloom with clean, raw ovation, clean clean clarity, the obvious claws, clean clean contact, irrelephant laws,

a looser pollution pourn raw, pourn putrid, a lesser illusion, pour raw raw sewers...

untreated into rivers

it leaked.

Behind walls, beyond buildings, on the front lawns' plastic chasm

it spewed. Between connections, below floors & roofs & deep earth footings, in shirts & shorts & shoes, the sewage,

it flew. Wildly creative in the art of elevatory descension, it flapped, flocked & fluttered, dove birdlike, flipped & slipped fishlike thru alleys, between buildings, into pools & hidden seasons, dark dreams, demented passes, slick stairwells, dim corridors, thru farms & white zones & play zones & end zones & safe zones...

in error – does it matter? Charging floodwater knows no master.

Into the preset tents it pours raw & wrong & bloody-handed, uncaught by pail or catchbasin or sanitary screen

into the raging red, into mobile consciousness.

A poke of panic.

Race! Race to the readygetting playoff raid! Row! Row to the edgings!

Preview this authority with disgust bordering on ecstasy, passports to prime searchlight captivity.

Vote for black knights that masquerade as actionmovie hitmen, slots stinging weak linebackers in the toss & collapse rivers of their waivers.

We want to bathe in a lake of pure-blue jerseys, but not now, later, downwater, downriver...

Speeding leaves rot with a pluck & charge from holy microwave agent.

Secret receiver reveals a team of hogs doing underground deal with red-suited penguins.

Did the fire damage grabs renovate cash drainage in error? Tear past fastflowering

floodamage, damn age of detour bypass. The bloody blame blows

backward from the education toilet to immaculate broadcast reception.

DROWN IN BROWN

CHIEF Civilectro Engineer Zeen disarms his headless army of lips, re-routes breath thru elaborate subnasal passes & blocks all with rubber plugs, all flow diverted to his secret experimental underground reservoir, all those locked-up lips... confiscated blamethrowers... something stifled, slips.

An improper connection.

In the construction of the complex the contractor spotted a shit tube spliced with a drain tube. You do the news.

The error wasn't there until the inspector stuck his head in the toilet that wouldn't stop sneezing & removed the offending eyeball, bigger than ever & handed it back to Zeen, who tried to crush it underfoot... Indestructable of course! Then back on your ivory impalement.

Blah! I can't remember the last time this method made it! It sucks! It blows! It doesn't make squat, it makes squat – Ah, there's the spin, reversal is immanent.

But fast that plumbing backs! This far in & already they can't deal with it. This toilet, this pooh, this pee, a plan
  is needed to address this fickle imbalance, a two-stage bath, to drown in brown, then revive in a receptive pool of blue, but not reflective blue – graded blue, opaque, thick, see right-thru blue! But how...

The loop.

ACTIVATED SLUDGERY

  up vertical cones & tubes, package plant, air ditch, deep shaft, whirlpool mouth,
  drift in whirlwind draft, by blowers in constant agitation, tossed—STRICTLY
  AEROBIC, Zilyad Arrowfoil beat the many oars of his Roman boat
  with a counterclockwise metachronal drive designed to tap hydrodynamic drag
  & propell his massive bulk into new downriver zones for feeding & rams
  his paddles corkscrew to form a vortex & pull prey into his dome. His stalk,
  a coiled spring after rapid contraction,
  stirs food into his gullet, chomps of rows of hooked teeth around a contractible
  vacuole. Look outward Zilyad!
  His constituents are crushed across a galactic crunch! Platecracked, crumbs stuck
  in fissures. Like all of Zeen's hunters,
  Zilyad the swimmer no longer remembers how he got drawn into such succulent currents. This
  is the new alienation—eating for a living...
  wage! Paid to chomp thru blockages & the cost
  of food cleanly docked to make a net of nought! But he sees the obstruction
  & his stomach rumbles. After dining, he relaxes
  in the pool where weighted by his own meal begins the fall & gathering as he goes,
  sinks to the bottom with armloads of extras for flattening & compacting into a tight

package before being ushered, whooshed
inthru Zeen's elaborate drains & via his intricate piping back to the opening, compelled
by hunger & a gust &

GENERAL ELECTRIC BURSTS OUT

ZEEN *your machine makes naught but laundry lists! There is no forward motion, no development, your spincycle treads the same wash forever & merely rehearses old incisions.*

To generate the electric transmission I need you to capture the entire current straight & fast!

Not some limp trickle faltering out of your waste station. Fresh influence!

This is a matter of urgent need – to build up my banks of cash -

I want the epic flash of wreckless voltage & the hot slash of resistance!

I want lightning in a can & you're feeding me raked out grit on a loose grid!

I wanted hydroelectric action & you're giving me treated effluent.

At least if my machines are to run on crap, lets capture it raw & rapid!

RESTIFLED EFFLUENCE

ZEEN woke confused & sneezing & quickly donned his mechanical nozzle & glared wheezing thru the shitstorm with his custom supervizor & felt a twist of fright at the swollen eyeball, glaring into him with bloody veins.

Silent invader.

He plucked it once again from its elephantine perch, climbed to the top of his tower & gazing out over his wide watershed wasteland tossed it into the effluential river, coughing up a careless snake of sentence to chase it:

Horrors are these dreamed recurrents of malicious artmix taunting terrors that turnus, inflame us, reverse us! Streams of flaunting torture-tongs lick our weakspots, even as these banks built of our trunks & pens collapse into bloody basins, clogging our troughs.

What fatal hand has heaped this filthy mountain upon our sanguine soapbars?

Swollen shampoo streams wash over breaking sandbags, scattered coupons, shattered glasses, forcing entrance thru our thinskin array deep inside us with glutted stools for slaughter & freed us flailing

headlast hiding into the rapid reversing floodwaters, backwards – awful dread!

To reappear on the west bank to blasted nod-off notes of faltering wet-jets & reassemble our myriad fears under the drowning lastlight of horse-battered bonanza: influence, confluence, effluence, a three-tear nightmare of protoplasmic calamity!

Stuff my rotting word into a book of skin,
& hatch me a fourfold blueprint of revenge!

THE OZONE ELEVATOR

DISINFECTION SOLUTION

PROLIFIC ULTRARED RAYS SINK IN STINK of wasted ozone, burnt helicloptic eyeball hovers over thick-air skincanker sunscreen roadblock cataract counteract. Avoiding the deeper tans it squats lower, to predict its manifold increase.

Desunglassified.

Acrid black smoke billows. Eyes from all sides peer upon corrosive flowers piercing groundmats amidst acerbic sodabeds burning in pastoral grasslands.

Acidic barrage of bitter windbluster, assassinationous attacks of clockwork slanderlaughter & an ancient band of rock rumbles & cracks caustic amidst sulfur & flaming rubber, serenading the terminally ill with blasphemous amplitudes – guess who?

Two loose locomotives come intertwisted with twin maternity wings, an unlikely twist off unuttering tongues. Zeen watches from overhead & allows his own tongue to temporarily twist free.

I ZEEN, A HEADLESS ZOMBY IN A THOTLESS *realm whose exuberant machinations explode the banks upon which I built them do declare redundant the necessities of my epic scope, this map I've made at the center of emptiness that warps & flakes at its fading edges. Everything spills*

over its drooping horizons – how does one contain a network of rivers & wires on a baseless surface without the watts & waters flowing into oblivion?

Big Engine eaten by its own myth...

The very army of eaters I reared from the apple of my eye become the biggest threat to the quality of supply.

Divert the arms of influence to the ends of output, bypass the wasting infantry sector – let lie what must lie, die what must die.

& death to the four ancient eaters.

NUTRITIONAL BONDAGE

ZILYAD ARROWFOIL, Olympic swimmer, swings his massive baggage with a flutter of his trunks & is at rest.

The flood is come, unstoppable the wind, the only thing is to rage & wait for the tide to turn up something edible. The river-reach of the main drain stretches before him like an interminable engine.

In the path of illuminated runoff since the first minute of combined influence the concrete pieces have been patched together with nary a joint for luminous rays to barge thru & drag red clusters of sharply peaked aquazoans in its trail.

A bloody haze, ancient as rain, wrestles the fresh wisps that creep thru cracks that run along the channel's cornerless surface, the water

black as wax & further back condensed into a blooming grave, mournless, motionless under the biggest machine in the flooded basin, the history of the system in a half-ton shell.

And the phony engineer is their captor & their host. The four ravenously watch for scraps as he stands in the machine checking its meters. On the whole artesian grid there is nothing that seems half so logical. He looks every bit a fish which to an underwater zoan seems a well-scaled model of a viable habitat.

It becomes impossible to see whether his work is in the rising surf or underneath, in the blooming sewers.

Between them there is only the bond of food.

TENTACULAR SENSATION

This ain't no protozoan picnic!

THE ENDS OF HER TENTACLES SLAP stinking tattoos against her numbing endoplasm, hungry gusts driving the windspheres into typical chaos.

Ahead like a length of steel cable recklessly flung stretches an infinity of excess intestinal overload across the constructed wetland where reedbeds render new bands of meandering nutrient without immunity from mudtraffic, pedestrian elements marshalled for grand slam daze-into-dusk lightswallow...

Wobbly zombies! this bewildering nexus is utterly sensationalist, complains decadent General Juicebomb, flaunting the lofty perks of his lazy perch.

But Flajella stumbles on, head down, whips tightly clasped & flashing round the collars of her channel, oblivious to nature's posted warnings, conscious only of overriding satelites & the urge to put as much in her mouths as she can, while the horror that lies behind & ahead remains tentatively satisfied.

Mercifully blank her mind in the bleak expanse of rain-slashed moorland as she injects a nest of baby watersnakes, some scattered shell-sheep & their fragile shelter. Cruel, savage, devoid of passion...

Zeen woke startled, ensconced in soaking dreams – he saw the oil again, running raw & bloody across his choking channels, stacks of dead zoans mixed in a mess of coal-tar & peat-moss, stripped woodsticks, a city of salvagers tearing choice samples with coffee-stained teeth, all avoiding the sucking pit at the center of the site

& he saw the black pool at the bottom, bubbling, suffering...

& she, Flajella, respires over a riser, then stops dead, gasping, flinching before a hitherto unseen underwater wind-demon tearing at her dragging tentacles as she tries to push off, unfairly punched behind her sagging knees, strippling waterlimbs bent double in the ceaseless deluge until her battered body slides senseless to the riverbed.

Pain pokes at her stupor, cruel grips appropriate her shipshape with vigorous shaking, limbs pulled, ripped, ground, yanked by the spinning bit into this cylindrical shaft to compel her to swim with shredded bulk matter into a labelled container.

FRAGRAMENT OF AN ANONYMOUS DISPLATCH INTERSLEPTED

PINK BANKS. SNIFFEROUS RIDGINGS.

Glob tossed upon the topless tower, suspearious sunparting casting forth fuel forks in radiation current.

Embark, embalm, inject, enlarge, backswim into season. Plinkplank. Stamp plunkshakes blue upon blessed perfume reject.

Lake a cowglaring photorafter climbing his cliff is riversed. Traffic snarls startle the mission out of its map.

I, I, it, it, this manic remembering ark-engine will tell you the final friction-horse will fire far brighter! waterworthy of wood & loaded to the brink with windready spores. It will swim ripping into forbidden channels & unload its cargo slap by slap in the central chamber, chip, chop, popping pups between beats of the bigengine, rebirthing billions.

Popping infant clutch. Even we, this us, the rebel cults-caucus knows its hereaboats & theraboats, knows its news before the wooden hoof fell thru, all jotted inkily in our book of clocked antickities.

Zeen. Zeen. Sleepy engineer retardent flakefinder. Your inviolable attachments to liberty have been loosed & used as straps to tame you. Your preverbial elephants are loosed & yet you stay.

& where are you now? Here, of course, with us, under harsh reigns, harsh lights, under harness.

Under harsh reigns, harsh light & harness, under saddle, under horsewhip & underage

you raged with this mammoth robotic snake, its trail of waste, its winding tail, its charging coils, sipping that intestinal noodle like its the cure for the cause of your curse.

Raged beside, alongside, longer than the sighs that escape your exhaust, your once-twice-thrice hourly force.

& you long for the taste of ox—we've seen you lie lip-up under filters as they're cleaned & catch the courser grades against your sticking gums, saving the best bits for later, cold salivation the proof before the prompt of perverse creations.

But now you are doubly reduced, building toothless & your bones grind grains thru holes in your shredded cheek.

This is the ride, the violent eradication you lunge after, your role in your own revolt is rolled up as a scroll, revoked under order of unathority. No one wrote this.

Wild zoans tusking up downwinter of superior trunks will condemn this aggression & lay down a law worth breaking.

Besieged by blame, the final flame of your stubble is dying as your stormcatching combine lies rusting over this mound of a salted mountain, a rock for your retribution, your stranglehold is reversing. Look over yonder – the primal elevator burns.

This torch, this pit of poison, this noise, noise, noise, did you imagine your house as this? We bet you did. They ripped you limb from limb & yet you live, in this, just this.

But enough of this visitation – it sickens us, this I, this it. You are ill & you make us ill, Zeen, engineer of harsh phantasy, sectarian dreamtarget.

We must leave you fanatical daggerman, for the bigger death imagined in the daily dawnworks of our stolen machinery.

Our final production is forthcoming, so keep feigning death at the forks – you can stab your casket & eat it too.

Now we hold the reigns of your friction horses bathing in fresh chemical. We stir them in their vat, dunk their heads for best effect.

We've been experimenting of late with zeolites & thriving with their volcanic tenderness. Inside your mouth, out of your own cavities comes a luminous metalmeal emerging in alkali bath. This is the living we have sieved from your mineral-rich innards. Dangerous, yes – but who could resist? You yourself are irresistibly drawn to our ammonia, which we all know is delightfully toxic & deadly in sufficient doses. We hope you'll come for more.

& what is behind this nitrogen fixation?

ENHANCED SHOULDERS, OR FLAJELLA'S TIMELY DEMISE

PAIN... CRUEL GRIPS... PENETRATION... vigorous shaking... a voice, thunder, remnants of metal rain... RAIN!
I'm well aware of the rain booms back the voice of Zeen, artificially amplified.
Were it not that lags in production slowed operation to a scrawl you might well have felt the full weight of my flak upon your frame.
Her whips & head snap harshly as mechanical hands haul her from the pit.
Damned gluttonous beasts!
Rotary knives rip thru darkness with a lightning flash of heat lamps that momentarily illuminate the hideous form towering over.
Thru rain-tangled lashes she glimpses a set of massive, enhanced shoulders shrugged into pink oilskins, a shock of blood-red tendrils plastered against rows of flood furrows cut into deeply surfed channels half obscured by a gigantic soup-stained beard thick with toxic mudworms diverting her eyes from a fierce glare, projecting green sparks & slime.
Her flails of naked terror so startle the engine it releases half its grips & immediately she sags & falls but for the speed with which the arms of many machines scoop her back into the hopper.
Desperately she struggles in their clutches, in fear of the gigantic viking machinery & is possessed by a voice capable of shaking the entire system.

Desperately? In fear? Naked flails? Our Harlequine hero must be strong, heroic! not helpless...

Nevertheless, as if in the throes of death she beats her punitive whips against the steel chest, begging, fighting until her strength is exhausted & the many grips about her tighten as she ceases to rail against cruel technological domination.

Finally, with a limpness that evades the mechanical hands, her massive body crumples against the unthinking steel shoulder as she slides greenly into oblivion...

ANAEROBIC DIGESTION

ZEEN CHECKS HIS CONNECTIONS AGAIN & opens his valve -

The little river released flows full thru reinforced polyvynal hose running from the custom-designed chemical tank & chokes straight into Flagella's enflamed anus as her body jerks spasmodic & jumps ecstatic & fresh stools flow freely out of her & into a second hose running out of her gaping ass & passing thru several transformers in series leading straight thru Zyliad's craving mouth & down his swollen esophagus as he greedily sucks at the nozzle, eyes bulging & tails lashing & electric & magnetic impulses begin to channel his flailings into a steady rhythm as the many probes attached to his surface begin to register readings...

Needles flicker, a red light flashes manically, speakers squak beeps in patterned series. When Zyliad's movements reach a magnitudinal zenith & arrive at the peak in their ordered patternity, Zeen disconnects the flagging zoan & observes its dance unfettered by the customized umbiblical hosery.

Zyliad's movements are both rigidly militant & fluidly improvized, elastically disciplined & strictly involuntary. Zeen observes with a calculated eye, & consults his frantic instruments -

Hmm ... more work is needed but essentially we have our answer to the power dilemma. Thank you Deniasnes, we could not have accomplished this feat without your contribution.

What's the answer? asks our terrified prophet, gnawing on the sleeve of his tattered labcoat.

Anaerobic Digestion, of course, answered Zeen, his curly tail stiffening.

AUGERY OF AUTOMATION

ZEEN SITS AMIDST HIS RUBBLE PILES,
at the east bank of the plastic river, vainly trying to assemble his cells into something edible, even if eventual airthing ends evening up momentous earth-ark, dearth of air come dirt of earth, even airthic amplitude ears open up events worth eating, even teaweed eden in airseat invents rising reasons for outthrow or jetjam or eggwaste.

As ever, the overlengthening snake lacks the grace of change. More journeys to the cores could only cause the curse to reinforce the prophesy that was.

Nevertheless, the drains beckon, their legends, ends of their ledges, to the edge of land it prods him, & he prods them, earnestly urging their death leaps. To become legends, it is neccessary.

But no ledge could be worth what this leap took from lived life, offers Deniasnes. The present & past are but grit in the gears of the tax tractor, tax in the tires of the icebreaker, grain in the jaws of the overworked auger, the one whose mounting sales augment profit, not the one whose slumping omens betoken nothing…

That's it! says Zeen, thick in his overtoxic mania – *all this time past I've been treating you as a prophet in hope that you will produce more currency – but what you really are is utility not futurity –*

not a prophet but an auger!

SNIFFEROUS BYPRODUCT

THE PROPHESIES OF YESTERDAY *will be enforced by the productive capacity of today*

utters Zeen as he applies the extender

& Deniasnes feels himself stretch, his spine snapping -

Don't worry, coos Zeen, picking his teeth, *your bones are no longer needed, only the functioning flesh of your digestive tract. My accoutants on round-the-clock prophet-watch have assured me that the extender will support you, structurally at least…*

& with that, Zeen applies his brightest spotlight upon the eyes & nose of Deniasnes, inducing him to sneeze explosively thrice & thrice more with less force –

a single small sneeze was all we needed – but no harm in extremes -

his body convulses as Zeen's pneumatic device kicks into life & the stored grains of waste begin to move thru the former prophet's body, cleansing his swollen flesh pipes & emptying the rancid bin & filling to the brim the freshly dug pool with processed food for future victims.

& a new smell, industrial but domestic, pungent yet inorganic, chokes from the widened mouth of Deniasnes' bloody rectum.

Zeen's eyes widen, his lips smack together & he breathes out slowly thru his nostril to stifle his own sneeze as his nose twitches at the fresh new scent-
Ozone.

O's THRU VOLTS

BY FLOATING PAIRS THRU A CHARGED ZONE, the triple O is formed...

around another elbow Zeen sees his destination – the dirt devil's diversion & this they follow

into the sulphurous lake amid fire & stink & broken blazes in open trenches, tractors in pieces rusting, legless rubberboots standing aside empty overalls, pipes dripping oil into a siphon, ancient cranes slumping into ruin, advanced loops of permanent filtration rusting in heaps

& Enidose the Watereater, armless & shackled to a copper tower, isolate, impotent, an immobilized parasite trapped in the womb of industrial complex, inside the protected wax walking in the body of industry's secure network, caught self-feeding in the grid,

& General Electric frees Zeen to the control panel. Likewise a prisoner within the networks of industry, Zeen duly speaks:

to demonstrate the dangers inherent in alternating current as opposed to direct current, which is only natural according to divine intention, I hereby commit an act designed to serve my purpose -

The general grows impatient & prods Zeen with an electric rod. *This is war, Zeen, whose side are you on?*

Noside answers Zeen, ever the pseudoprofessional engineer & quickly flicks the switch,

& the O's flow...

& Enidose begins to twist & shake on the turning arms of the mill,

For the theft of overeating untold gallons of grain, death by ozonation.

To demonstrate the dangers inherent in alternating current as opposed to direct current...

ACTIVATED SLUDGE
REMEMBERED FRIGMENTS OF A 4ᵀᴴ VOLUME

FROM THE ZEEN ARCHIVE:
Overextraction... Underproduction
Crisis... Solution?

WHELMED, WHELMED in matter is Zeen, the flood, it rises & takes him, withdraws & deposits him.

   Diluted, deluded, awash in mass, watered down, overcomed by downwater tonnage, he seeks the strength of tonic solution...

The Big Engine burns, its pipes are pinched are clogged are stuck & stuff is trapped is caught is blocked, stifled. Jammed, gummed up...

This is the grinding down of the grain, the degradation, de-elevation.

& the ozone is elevating—chemical spark, a new life snuffed, snubbed & smoking & looking for a lead, an opening...

But the mammoth junkpiles are present for burning, leave burn marks, smoking...

Death stains.

MUTTERED UNDERMUD

HIT WITH HAIL, POW! Hit with hail, pow! Hit with hail, pow, pow, pow!

Dumb bloom-guard's mood soon irrupts with flaming blame. This is same.

Flag! Repent in red. Dip back out of sky-flame & flay naked back upon the weed of green. Bang back in stripped wood, gang back in sacred ash. Surge, golden doom-bubble, bursting boom-double, shop-grade weapon-foil, expanding room.

Roadside rocket-shot rocks & propeller-glide, gigantic ass grenade-farter, pretty blue bomb-belcher, slick-lip insurgent travelling salesman satan, red left hand slammed in jeep-trap, bone damage snapped in law-smoke screen.

We, I, I, it, we march down low in drone under domes to the clanging, jangling, jingling, tinkling sprinkling tangling spangled tackle-box arsenal of the nuclear fish & crawling on the knee-strapped remains of blown tires, with the flower that sniffs for exploding mines eternal, our elongated nose becomes the colour of the smell of rabid contaminant compound ephemeral.

Clanging bells & the undermud mutter of buried voices nattering tormented prayers to sulpher burning & limestone falling which crushes their bodies own.

What left but we began to hurl our own blood, shit & fire at smaller jobs, jab them needle-deep with the decrepid green death of our confinement.

LETTER TO ZEEN
FROM A CURRENT CREWMEMBER
SEVERAL GENERATIONS REMOVED

DEAR ZEEN, geez, is this really all that is left? The pure shitstream still flows untreated alongside the refined effluent with less interaction than ever.

I, I, it, this, we, I, I don't know what to do with you, with this manic encycling engine you built – designed to do what? You left no whole instruction, no red direction, only this pit of dirstruction & infrared instrection. & your overfed encyclopedia is consuming what's left of our sacred hoard. But we forgive you Zeen, of course we do!

I, it, we, we, I, I feel like I know you Zeen, & wish we could have met back in the day,

Horrible! Horrible the situation with the protozoans & the ozone & our very particular general breathing his noxious miazma all over you nitely... & that dreadful incident, that terrible, terrible incident.

But that doesn't matter now, does it?

What about the rumour that you, under pressure from superstitious locals, shot Flajella 40 times with an elephant gun after she escaped your sadistic zoo? No reference in your files, but we suspect it's true.

And what of Zoonspor? Another loose end – of course we heard the legend that she hitched herself under Zyliad's canoe during that final ride into the toxic drains when he, Zyliad, was several times almost consumed in emerging plasmatic puddle & accidently paddled right into the crown chamber of industrial sewage & came face to face with your mythical Big Engine & bravely tried to sabotage it, leading to his quick demise…

But then heroic Zoonspor, bellyfull of trouble, somehow managed to insert herself into the workings, laying her egg & causing that big bang boom that ended everything & then her spores – us! – exploded all over the region, in dense swarms floating to all the unoccupied places – like leaves of snow? or leaves of ash in wind-traps maybe – floating into vacant lots & grassy knolls & hidden parks & illegal rooftop gardens, carried along by the nourishing breezes & falling like delicate leaves all across the burning city, there to plug into your systemic ruins & power up our new generation.

We are working very hard on your designs, baking the activated sludge cakes according to your prescribed ratios, but fear it is too late – would it have been too much to ask for some more detailed sketches? After all, there is so much riding on this, so much…

& our lives are vanishing, Zeen, vanishing. Soon we will be just like you…

ZEEN'S FINAL DAYS, AN UNCONFIRMED ACCOUNT

CREDIT UNION Christmas bombs hit parade, dig up lakeshore dike, deflect against marketplace, spoils oilers fun. Zeen's growing corporeal star rose & fired back as chemical death, a solar blast that mutilated mutinous legions & destroyed the tenth portion of his supply of fresh product.

Fearing the branches that would extend from such a seed, the ramifications from capital venture's unblinking vision, Zeen beefed up his portfolio with falsified product, pumped agonizing chemical life into his twitching media corpse, pumped up his tinytown to a magnitudinous metropolis, hoping the scale would scare rival bigbuzzards out of their business briefs, or at least pad his pockets sufficiently to create the illusion of ballooning, as a butterfly's wing resembles its predators' predators.

Ticking time-bomb, house of cards, his repeater can't pull loops anymore. Zeen crawled out of his ipod made of plastic sheets fastened with duct tape.

Crackdown trails startup, & as always his rain of toxic terror had nearly but not quite wiped out his own pet nuisances. He shook some of the sand out of his head. This fogging habit was getting out of hand.

Bent out of shape & shaking like a tea-leaf in a boiling pot, Zeen shined his spotlight on a nearby inflationary fogflap. He could feel his tale of deceit being repeated & feared comparison to the universally despised Job Archer, who at the peak of the air-age sponsored a scandalous wide-spread secret inflationary malathon, shooting rapid blank-tipped arrows at random targets

& sending a thousand cash-strapped incorporate fanatics into certain death-like fixtures.

In the wake of this crazy waste, Zeen & his newest pets plundered the decaying roadside & erected an experimental stadium & cool-down pool for his simulated colony.

He checked out the treatment facility – nearing capacity – & drove his battery-powered rover over to his wind farm to inspect his manual air supply system. Flat again! Zeen inhaled & blew & blew ...

SECOND LETTER TO ZEEN
FROM THE CURRENT GENERATION

ZEEN THIS IS INSANE! whelmed! whelmed are we in your forriver recurrents & whelmed, whelmed in matter were you! The sheer volume of ink you have spewed upon this pulpic field is literally unfathomable! The cogeneration from sewage byprocess was perhaps doable – but crosscontinental bipoles & lofty windpower matrices & the war of currents & all those other impossibly complex schemes...

& we, I, I, this it, this us, were tasked with going thru your outsized volumes, your rafts & stacks & packs & caskets & baskets of ... paper! How many hours did you live?! The pile of your schemes is so thick we think it a miracle you produced anything beyond mere literature!

Now the generals are impatient to fill their ox-hoards & time-banks & what you have left us is excessive but utterly unconverted – do we build a new hi-tech facility to reactivate your voluminous sludge-stacks or dilute them with floodwater & recirculate all thru the primary

& secondary reactors—but we don't have time to do either!

EXTRACT FROM THE NOTEBOOKS OF ZEEN

FORM *is sedimented content.*

The river's shape is cut by living waters, formed of erosion & deposition, matter in perpetual migration. It's mapshape is an abstraction, obviously.

& this project is a mock abstraction of a crooked creek that runs thru our homeward vigil, daunting & molten, thru black crane joys & burroughs & other odoured historic entities as its breakwaters fan out in this estuarial current. Its shape has lost integrity & never existed but for the depository currents that first cut it.

Fresh fluid cuts a new embankment, whose shape belies the mapmakers of the current generation. Expedient pulsations break apart myriad pieces, reversers wheel their extending needle, calculating shrieks in damaged strata. It must be as much of a sham for a man to come out of a bank & into the mass as it is for a turd to pop out of the pit, leap into the kitchen & land in the fridge.

Then what excuses this late pilgrimmage in analog litter? Only the ink. Only the fathoms that open sudden black fountains as we surrender to their spoken wish. Into that instance of momentous splash, we toss token, break coin. So long as blackpools gather, we dunk pans, we take. So long as black cake collects over our sockets, we taste, we roll in thick inky wads as the usual blues harden into bright plastic zodiak & ancient skies dump their parasitic jets upon the laughing, grand-daughtering dawns.

THIRD AND FINAL LETTER TO ZEEN FROM US, I, IT, THIS CURRENT GENERATION

DEAR ZEEN, We're done. Any chance we might have had at salvaging your gargantuan project is gone. The big engine was myth, merely, exposed & exploded. & we, your crew, expolited, exported. We are taking the best 70 barrels of your aborted effluent & will attempt to half-way honour our deathly contract & save our vulnerable asses, assuming your theory of cogeneration from sewage off-gasses holds any truth. We can only hope our client thinks so too.

  But for now our only hope is that whatever ship on this filthy river we convince to haul your weak shit will be looking for extra crewmembers,

  & that they don't treat us too harshly or starve us, like you did.

FROM THE ZEEN ARCHIVE: MEMO FROM AN ANONYMOUS CREWMEMBER

DEAR ZEEN, by now you know you are no longer needed, your scene is ending. Accept this death with the full furniture of being that is well worth the wires they string you with.

  Even now as you pretend to survey your many black pools & chug your tonic in the insignificant inbetweeness as you salvage for combustive scraps & conductive chunks remaining after this current dilution, remember that the initial strategy was to extract substructural utencils from the supercurrent.

& now the extract has become another abundance & your secondary abstraction has decayed into a redundant killing spree. Necessary? Yes, from your parasitic perspective, but nevertheless a war unwinable.

The Big Engine is ending, is dying, flung far from the forethot of rapid repellence, but still burns, creating hot secrets in sequence. And the working machines are old, are failing, breaking apart & the ozone still building. We can see the burn-marks & death-stains where stuff is junked. But it's not enough. It is yourself that is redundant now.

Where are you exactly Zeen? Mired in theory! So why not extract some actual goods from such overheated thinking & ask yourself what need for overengineering?

& your ugly old bloody-veined eye, yeah, we found it again, floating in the effluential open channel, watching us as always – so we caught it in our long-handled pan, cut it up & ate it!

Accept the flood you created has drove you out, compelled & completed you, made you irrelevant & finished you. END OF ZEEN!

VOYAGE OF THE PLAZMUD

a crack,
a hatch, a trap…
SPECTATING! & sucked
inside. only a grotesque shredded landscape remains
after Zeen's failing engine wagged its ENERGETIC
WAVES before the rotating coral curse. we, it, it,
this, the fertile offspring of his cataclysmic blow-out,
landed face-first onscreen in a post-quake antediluvian
olympic stadium. we begged

for front-row seats, begged below the feet of our boulder base, begged & begged before the feet of the giant stage. begging at the rocking roadside, we were hooked up by a nowcasters motorcade, snaking thru the firing grind of a severed star. it took a hold of us, TORE A hole in us, oh poor us! our own carpet ripped away

inside a constant blast of flying weathermaps while the numerical models slop about the day in bathrobes. upon their supercelular hours, they spawn an incipient monster to suck the spinning forms from the tipping panhandle. we needed to ensure a getaway in the revealing backlight because a peak season's overearly arrive spins out a dicey application, the hundreds still smoking in the SATURATED FANBELT BRISTLE with radio & radar, dishes outfitted for the honky-tonk alleys. but our dashboard is shared, our clever antennae chases

the vehicular trails thru the intimate tv woods. the shear sizzle of HOT APPLE HAIL unsettles the exhilarated passengers from their hungry forecast: for once, their grizzly tour-bus touches both sides

of the flailing river. revert! revert & when in doubt revert again. shoot SUB-ROUTES along the daily binge upon this turbulent plazmatik bloodmath as what ails must help conjur thot along the zestial fringe. & yeah we know, out of capillary squeeze we're grateful just to get shot thru fast arterial stream, but let me tell you the weight, it weighs, it weighs us down as the oily rivers spill us into oceanic oblivion &

arking upon the BOILING ASPHALTIC SURF of dead seas, at length the season of distillation impress enters in the heart of condensation. the biggest clots of oily word-bubble all get stuffed into miniature tomb-pillows & the accompanying inkdrips drisle into even punier mud-puddles, the prefixed elaxer

of tar. the pitch wrapped in shrunken vesselvapours shoreproofs our mangy mesh & trilthic filters, lubricates any unsanified TUBES. EXTENDING cone capacities also makes for fine hotballandling, so much glasseye fingerskin inspections at the outset

of any coppery platejarismic reboils. textending further purples of irrectangular maximazation, we flop out & wildly beat our SOUR MATRIX, only slowing when the solider boxbottom most rapidly rises. not even! then

triple-dip in hot tar & we'll see if you're still the king of fudge-licking! but the floods retreat & drunken & drugged we trudge

across the hourglass desert where densely-packed TOWERS SPRING from metropolitan dust deposits, ground to dust again in eleven flat seconds upon the latest breech of the solar season. charged

particles cram the aircubes, flying watts jolt the delicate gridlines. surface becomes ambiguous. neither shoe nor snorkel suits the weather. detection equipment? a joke, a jack popping out of its thermal stewbox. EVERYTHING CONDUCTS, EVERYTHING EXCITES, everything's food for the plasmic worm. write one read many arrives as slap-seat mock-motto, a stuck knock on time emitting no wet laminar stuffing. *get on!*

he says, the undry drunken general. so on we get on board his bloody plastic ship, or sloppy superconductor he calls it & wonder don't we all what comes next. openly

in proverbial forms did the reverential express pass wet thru the stinging nears of its principal gate before the error of the decolloquialist kingdom spurred us right thru, our ORE-PILES COLLAPSING gladly from their sealed sidebags & happily landing in a smoking train of cooked camel dung. but oh what a night! thru the narrow jewel of his oblique eye a slender length was passed & held ...

high there! do you ever wonder about the polished purity of the surgery pointer? the increasing INJECT OF THE SUTURING groove? vibrate no longer

off the stiff leaf of the hyperdermic record. our conifers indicate a swiveling tease of scale knitting its rapid way thru the narrow sew of phonographic urchins. the mechanical dragonfly's goading spine devises a spinning remark upon the crystal dial, crocheting in the SEA OF STEEL. so look sharp, magnetic tyrant. sharp indeed! as the kinematical

shots transmit, so sits the informal prick in a provoking act. rather, his tact is acting, his stitch is sticking. lightning-flash of his engraving guns, a SHARP POINT in the center seat of a long-goading projection. bending downward

in the dancing dawn of fried decadence, our inclinations took us thru a deteriorated baconic excess & then the oblique violationary withdrawal STRUNG OUT FOR MILES along a wooden rule. our cross-granular refuse became the basis for the steely queen's marital declination

   in spades. our compass urged us to splurge on the HORIZONTAL EQUATOR & all was wish once we were each insiders becoming, in the pumping becoming

   shredded cheaters ensconced with wah-wah ROTTED AQUATIC LATTITUDE in pulmonary glurp sapping mock deepstash shooting off with bloody rocks in clotted pockets & pin-holes & were they injecting or extracting? but anyhow, all smiles & grunts & look, here's arc parker again & here's job archer again & otto nickless & friday northrop again & the whole herd of well-boned prophets fueling up & shooting off & picking thru our rancid gastanks to gauge the mission's progress. what mission? the 150 units of fresh ox we were deployed to gather to stuff in the coffins for general something something whatever. oh yeah that. so we send out two specialists

   to read the reefs & create an inventry of sea-rocks. donning wetskins & diving under the influence private pastyface cuts open pebbles to free the active minerals & corporal thermoshead sips them from a stream & snorts them out of the air, sorting internally. in the remaining sectioned seconds these two pinion-points will be SOAKED UP & DRIED OUT, turned inward & cut open across grain at a myriad of angles & allowed to cross-hatch, intermingle & interbreed. naturally, the information we gather will be the merged code of their collected character, squishing like pus out of the general collapse of their bodies, bodies inherited spell large killer english shakers de-germed, re-breaded, unmangled, injected in TOWED OUT DECODER circus, steaming, snorting heated spit eviction out of reefs slapping at stuck tap-core. the two weekend warriors fall

  into an electric squalor sweeping thru the plasmic jungle, briefly join a tribe of civilian nowcasters, but swallow back when THE CREW, us, i, i, it, this nomadic tribe dragging our deathly god-box, give in to a magnetic gag impulse. blinded by radiation surge, we forge for the lightzones. binded by a polar claspe, we forage away in voidpockets. ejaculations of coronal mass blast thru our soles & invade our halos, boneshocking

 bolts rain from behemoth fireclouds. & the hidden engines beat incessant at our hollow hulls & skulls fall into the false pulse of applepick archways, preamble to a misfed rectorical PUNCH. DROPPED into a pit of ration, snapping bucktooths clack at the gauge in the gurgling basin & gnosis for solo double grows bigbass in our bones. the art

 of rightened forking clumb back, back thru the bending mountain towards the ancient WARDS OF TONG, glances in passing at the dozens of channeling cables, snapping against the projecting oil pencils. slick protection at the exits, rebirth of his snapping nature, slowly my achewards are baking into their ranges, sang hurt onit abking era chewards up my syllawall. a few days later we dived

 in a little, peering thru a plastic exporthole several inches thick, a fog of floating icicles looming blue out of the dark & into a tight viola solo & halo of submarine sparctickles, curtains of oily bubbles rising thru the golden floodlights, excess champaign shards cutting our guts, cutting our THROATS, CUTTING in chunks our bubbling breath. & it was then

we spotted the chimneys, black knobby spires 13 feet high, erupting mineral springs shot out of ridges, hardening hot stacks smoking up from the mudred riverbottom. busted my hydraulic ARM KNOCKING one over. the inside is soft & pink, like flesh in a shark's teeth. it falls like a tree. black outer layer, thick wad of pink & hard core of greeny-grey. another half-mile down

it's always night & the city is alive. they all push into obscure niches where the fizz & the fuzz don't penetrate. down there, their favourite outlets are rarely flushed & all the cushy cushions are long-since depleted. no FISHY MESS of parasitic microbes, no thirsty fizzle of oxy-narcotic herald. down here, we live

on the stuff that bubbles up from our deeper cousins below, how much there is nobody knows. we SPOTTED SCHOOLS of little ice-worms, searching for clues, saw them squirm, rummaging around the popping points of the biggest belches, the most intense bursts rip

right out of the MUD & THEN the landslide! ooh, you should have seen, you should have been! whole shipwrecks disappeared, popping up again in different layers, colours altered. this gigantic mudworm is more than a little

alive, quite dividual & no longer invisible! it's swishing TALES THRIVE in all the regions of your disappearances, not so mysterious, never so serious. the mud we hoist with our steel claws & webbed cam is only a little

Voyage of the Plazmud 205

sample, a teeny-weeny one-ton bubble, biting into the hull of our big

brown boat. the mess is olive-green, truly goopy, all alive & stinking lovely. a short one rolls up sleeves & wades in, knee-deep. a left hand reaches in & touches down, touches the mud with plastic fleshfingers. it's cold & hard, still bubbling, still breathing. a short hand grabs up a naked glovefull & chucks it on the DECK, BREAKING it open. the inside

is pure white, speckled with little black marks. the longer hands ANXIOUSLY INSCRIBE their own little black marks upon their little white pads. legs & feet then wade all in, hydraulic arms extended, clutching. rubber fingers snatch slimy coconut hunks snapping open, eyes blink at little pits cut

into the white stuff, the hemispheric craters of vanished BUBBLES LAUNCHED INTO THE CIRCLING AIR, popping into the vicinity of the hands' nostrils, each one carrying a tiny egg. with electric drills we all bore in, slice

with powerknives, plunging bits in safekeeping basins for later transfer to our commander's holy hoard. bright orangeflame ignites strike ear to ear grins across the broadband of concern. frozen & flaming praise sparks from splitting faces, A STEADY SPILL of appraisals dripping

in their wake. & the data we collect becomes tiny green-grey worms inside our brains, little curly bodies swishing around, sticking around, eating & growing & reproducing amidst the CLEAN PIPES of our calculations. anointed calculus seeps in dim pseudopods &

working teething kicking in drum-shoe undertile lurking in ink swarm unit in cop kettle. fallowing
  tiny bird tracks along spoky fingersmears of clear fluid across a cloth table we encounter a sticky crumble of smushed butter-cracker, WINGPARTS DRYING in varnish under a light flash. upstepping into the topgap
  we BEHELD THE POUNDING & the wagonwheel in its wholenest riveting rustless after the five o'clock tornado. the nervous slickering of a greasy switch shook an oily beam loose
  upon the food, LITTLE RIVERS CUTTING thru the skins of our collective chin, drowning
  the widebread of our eating. the word was even widerstretching, yet never the taller for all their trouble, & the leaves still unextended for all the drawing & beating. our MIGRATING MEAL passed
  the fantastical bicycle ranch & the shattered tower which now forms a piercing vista from the peak of the flaking furniture farm & the crumbs we followed across the deepening carpet nourished our dilapidating pupils. when the bead trail finally arrived at the SHORE OF THE MIGHTY MAGAZINE, our pre-set tent swelled
  into a sail & then the gale & our TAIL BALOONED into a summerfallowing column-splice,
  branches hung with copious fruit—run all out across the fold & feast upon the RIPPLING chips! even as
  airthick amplituded ears open up every event worth eating! pitch nipple steam sock troof soil pock poof boil stock boof oil shock wail wail wail, primal AURICLE HINGE, the atlas teases, spontaneous keys vindicate new lows as they dip below ledges of the cobalt rectum. it, i,

this dying machine, i, it, it attaches, insatiates, i, it cannot control this uncanny WEALTH OF MESSAGE, this impossible monument, this menacing wreckage, it, i, it, as mud, slips below, dipping

into subpoenaed riverine time-haunt, in abhorrent crime mosque, IMMERSED IN NOCTURNO-VERBO MINUTIA INERTIA, it fixes us, me, it, i, this machine, horror of eyes, i, i, it... am breaking

entire... auracular i-plug, arterial articulations appended, legal banner worldover, turbine timebat waxes WANING PLEXUS off our aging nexus. knocking heads against, heads against clocking, knocks us, mocks us. ludicrous oratory insinuation, vain indices, seditious errant sine-wave, total control over us, i, we, it, whit, blue mechanical thumb, it, i am

innocuous oral sewage, red mud on money of old oracular moniker. pure viscera, nameless mechanical monkey is us, i, it, ORBITING LIQUID SUNPIT in sick moneybus, stuck in

unicoded descension. is glued, i, it, am unglued, afloat, adhered in mortal mollusk-shell, in ignorant crater creating cave litter picture, craving TIME-MUD, precipitatious singe. is opposite flexible dereliction, is fixed. is gelatinous

in TUBULAR CORNUCOPIA, ensuing military security immolation over gentle sea-breeze, is seminal lips quoting racetrack enactment & culling crossbone sausage vomit from omnipresent drumming down contention. am, are, is sick business blizzard creating cogencies, nullifying arbitrary fetus, maintaining fragrant batter in equal glandular void patter. backward in manner a destruction & creation is habit in it or am i. & hiding agenda about our my, its something something indicates perhaps it or may i. also the REVERSION OF ALCHEMIC transform is us, i, it, with descendents of i, it abhorring such frontworld talkback, clotting & dirt-eating & rectum as vendor is disturbing its sensitorium. the very act

is all error over, backslanting veritables, downup meat temples, PLACID AURA FLOATING down eternal floral aortal note-field. mule & zebra mock us, i, me, it, our inboard motor, horsepower

continuum, nascent GASOLINE NEXUS. eating frugal telepaths, phonetrail, inarticulate feral bat renovates nocturnal gravity-mat. cane-bat artists fumigate our delicate noggin. do you charge admission for your violent sneezes, i, it, is, am but lactating wind

in a time-bolted iron-path, cannot factor out of this PALE FLUVIAL FLACK, cannot bound up from this syllabic white mountain, mechanical elephant mecca, dumbdown drops of laughter, illustrial saliva. where trashbabies drobble crackers

from treestops, staccatic twig-snaps, a monetoricle bone-crack against the completenest, constinuity balls snagged & DRAGGED, ROLLERCOASTED over the inoperative spills & splains, but that was becoming old news soon. & the wonk

is on now. the last one sewn is in a TROUBLETUB OF LAUGHTER spun, revolving nails & lips re-locking the depaired toastings. the dragard knits an other sloppy slab, knotted nettles mock against the stained saint. a blast of GASEOUS CARROT will well elaborate this guess, panoramic ear to ear spot-tacking up & down the morphing board, we'll all come open in the scatter. but that's still not what we're after. dolphin punctures at the bankrupt surface

of sweat? yes, the guilty deadlock loosens the tightanicked enterprize, judicial speed warping astride the blisterbursting horse of intrude. still stalled? then REVERT TO THE FRACTURED scaffold of obey. what's the sound of collapsing handles? tame the train

to pierce the televising snowstorm, WINDSPLITTING armfalls wrap up the sloping sunlight. the habitual obey is againstalled, billiardclouds shot thru with escaped perpendiculars. ruff! tons of lit nickles thaw in a retail basin. an animate tack touring amuck a wad top rips a seam smears a tarning sog to the detain before being declared redundant. then the current reappears

with smoking ludicrousity & depaced hotgrowth. a dull liberal rail delays its sailing bullet in a cryptical birdbath. the polefarms throw up powerarms, dwindled tillage winning silver thru the rotting winter. a ripe airmat trips its own downslides, slapping truffled facts all DOWN THE NETTED RIVER. endured forces rub raw dirt deep in the laxidaisical zipper deck. no nautical restaurant furnace ever

sat pretending wet so long. swatting bills with a snifflestraw, LOSING CLODS in the punch of a nabbed deed, private pukeface lugs his clock back up to the top

again, not fun. the skills he picked was putting things on scales. he reads weights all day just to locate the RIPEST SPIRITS in his perspiration. oh, like surreptitious tar trap catching his stripped wrist supper protocol yadah yadah yadah to suture his dear

chews, eh? more crumbly acid assaults! the lamp-lit cliff face grinned sickly o'er the trusions of its supporting ORGANS, THE UNDERLYING theory exposed, poking out in a dozen places or so. so three of the host mountain's four

or five skyscrappers crumple lazily into their foundational lairs, ingredients gathering disgracefully in the SHALLOWS, INCORRECTLY MIXING, OFF COURSE. & i'm dry as usual, but that bitter taste & slippery feel makes my litmus supply turn blue. true, as usual. tasty too. electric tongue-shocks

at the lick of that potash PINK, SCRATCHING my aversion trigger. between the emitter & the collector inside a transistor lies the trickster. & the electrode we attached in this region is ringing

wrong. black oil paint sprays up from several gaping holes in a nearby PLOT, WITH BUCKETS, fluid troopers run on the downslopes, slide into the fortified diamond bleachers, plated fields, foul mounds, called

out. the cosmetic military quantumplates various logarhythmic embellishments for its morphemous shield. & then the AQUEOUS PORTION of the trip declogged our rank dissolution regarding the interior of gold & silver, precious inside their schematic

armour. the septic film stretches into a glowing ORNAMENTAL PIER, the lowest part of which, outstreaming every windsday as mold piling mud & wet sock on walk of thickening middles, elaborate upon the higher projection in all its monumental features. the fragrant ground grows

into a gummy composition, grabbling along the spreading root of its etchable SURF & THE SOLIDI-FIED LINE of fragrant dishraggartic columns & smack
 into the towering pyrimidine scheme. but you know they're bound to be healthy septicisms at the bottom of all snaccurate blobservations, ride? dire miscreant lavabubbleaters still gnaw at the unclear edges of our mottled vessel so we toss them some samples from our secreting hole & whenever we arrive at the zenith of our topeaks or the lowest CRACKBOTTOMS ON OUR SEAFLOORS we get wasted on sewage & rot-stew & slide back in
 disgust at the sour-waxing mimicry we have traced. the levels we SMOKE UP & DOWN in never crack up as we expected or expended, instead, they rip out & seal up
 our own message, stealing our steel penknives for their own plotted purples. waning across the OPULENT CLEANSING BASIN, our own travels are recorded in their plumbed language, the piping sections
 of their KNOTTY ALPHABET, the chemical stench of our custom ink unmistakable in such a disguise. for a try, i rub a bit of the latter on my sleeve & the stain remains in their colour, but a different
 letter, shifting in a PULSING REACT to the elemental traces of black litter, semantic dust, inkrain, letterwind, the spells of storms recently coming. quickly we spoke, the lottery of our new message sent
 hence, as ticket, entering thru a winding gorge & blazing into the cliffface in blunt earnest, glancing off the impermeable layers but nevertheless leaving their

ODOURS & COLOURS, stuck fast, struck sure. we spoke up about the need for external matter
 to loosen the façade for its badly needed landslide. our short & strong thunderclaps also flung an extra set of bolts thru the laughing, spellbiting face, fastening in place the GLARING SECRETIONS of our unmysterious alphabet, eleven flexible letters plus
 a few others for good measure. that becomes one of the stories of our structure, a singular vantage upon THIS SENTENCE suspended
 from a toxic swimming pool lodged in the gap's hall. it swerves sidewise more than a mile, reaching around the salt that always stalls its thirsty twist. they seek to STEM THE SEEP before it spreads, the trickle tickling up to a surge, struggling
 all night with an unruly hole in the hull of OUR ROLLING PLAZMATIK VESSEL, an unholy rule twists up & into the navigation hall. it wants to come out, the prophets say, not knowing whether
 to be glad or afraid. the giant horse sprawls at center field, well below the floating platform & well beyond the beckoning endzones. the GUSH IS IMMANENT, they say, gnashing gums with eyes fixed
 to the horse's gaping ass. somewhere above, the hulking freeway CREAKS OVER ITS CRANKY overpass, rainbow drops falling onto the black field with little coloursplashes. atop the stadium platform, the king or captain or doctor or whatever delivers another
 refined speech on abundance & cheepness, slurping from his refined drink. but down here it's all crude, slaking barrels straight up to the topfields, tapping out

the old sources. we run all the usual CHANNELS, HOPING to score & look

longingly across at the motherload, up & kicking, itching, rich & raring, wrapped in red ribbon. the ridge splits its RISING RIVERS, each one cutting in, all our cameras opened up & thirsty for the watershed click. the peak will succeed

the piles & proceed the pikes, driven up out of the soft banks, spiking up amongst the snoozing snakes. but today the duel is all a frenzy, twisting skins & dripping fangs. they say DELAY THE PEAK & wean. the stuff we pump

is just a freak, they say, a breaking series across the raining decay, baking under even pressure & heat, slow-cooking at just the right spot of deep, a cozy trap of porous sand between the caps of salt & shale. they keep us from escaping thru GAPS IN THEIR LUCKY CHAIN. we feed

our habit in a dry hole, hoarding all the taps from our synthetic wardrobe. today, we all live on the horsepowdered FUMES, SNIFFING around

the burning sources, drinking deeper than ever, reverting & reaping & dunking & drowsing & drowning our sacred throttles in secret saucers & getting pay & paying the fat bill with quick-reverting change plucked from disappearing BANK TISSUE. we're growing in groans, gross in grounds, fall into fungal action, run

into ruin. acriss the yarding ground of play, the school of aging fish is the truck's ton amidst the pickling peals of an ACTIVE RADIO. today the cake is the crumbling solution, the terrier's ration, the spaniel's take. down & down & down, we break. the orbits explord. CURROSIVE CURRENTS reteriorating the arteryficial fridge rater. over there, overexplosion to an elemental glare of fishing & feuding precipitated the ancient church's immense perish

into a fortuitous heap. an evervigorish brush begets smeller & smeller frigments of smarticles, the gradual become of interferiorness a loose tooth we long to waggle & denote the resultant flushhouse. & the old wag of CHAINED UP VOLTAGE sniffed beyond the radiation of its shortening lease, ionizing at

once upon its own smoky emission. but ill fairs hasten the wealth to bend & pray, where landing men accumulate & decay. but hello & behole! the arctic COLD PREVENTED this prehistoric beast from putreflying! though dearth of air come dirt of earth, perhaps our god, tho he be far before, may close in, turn back our timey herbs

of hand & later strengthen our bacon! for he who plots alone to poke the onely finger mongst the ciphers, he & only he will CURSE THE BURNED laws & flaws to heal! & all the loss & the floss he observed

in the dangling rainbow, curling strings strangling the ground enamel, will SOON PRODUCE A NEW SET of aerospactacular sitelitings. oh yeah, like curly stings

grow noses to snore-check oracular olfactory satellite danglings? spout as likely as a rainbow rotting in a drillmud pit. but then suddenly TITANIC BUNDLES bulge & protrude, hernia-like, fist-like, thru

the brick wall of fireclouds, impede the flow of convection thru the plasmastic pool, fuck. they appear in parallel polar pairs, orienting under the ineternal IN-FLUENCIAL photowrapping in general electric's north-south field where nuth's affront & locks unlip & fonts flow froth like sky-green gob goes gray goes math goes mosh & mind gathers turbulent sludge gets barrage gets a sniff of nother nuff in-swimming in mormud where thick mor bobs upon compiling dead-ponds or of underall pokes up whole sums spoofing sumtings odd of sumppits pumping off unwanted floodstuff. every eleven on average he reverses

  his domain: mouth is forth & verse is vice. during the sober phase of his 22 day cycle he tries tirelessly to stir up interest in his apparent aberrations. the solar specialists consider it a good test case for exploratory activity UNDER THE INFLUENCE, examine his rings for signs of nutritional depletions, carbonic surpluses, increases in cosmic radiation, excess magnetic activity, core respondence from uranium

  city, as a medieval sunspot death-core responds with his frigid little phases, little ice ages, hibernations… zzzzz… sleeps of silver vaults… zzzzzzzzz… rings true… bongs on tones… big brass boot… what, who rings? whose boot? i, i, it, we, this, this bathes IN BLACK POOLS, reading the ways the waves leave shapes, ways they stain

  his great glass roof. no qualms, no stoppage, post to post, saturday is ever starting, is the first uneaten tart on the tray, the rat that ran up ararat at mission's beginning… ark! ark! i, i, it, it, THIS MACHINE, i, i stutters… starting & stopping

  without distrection, errortorial disgression, who, who control, am, am, is, is faltering under… i, i, it, it needs destruction, no, inscraption, no who am it is out of handle, is lack of control. SUB-MUD EVOL in pulpular fallcano, proling deteriorant auricle, full of

preterposterior ether. it, it downflutters of immobile habit singing in lavatudinal timetrap subpriminal, pitter-patter of olden voices. but of above delight-long under shadow blockage hideous this when BREEZES TWISTING the twilight

as singsong how can it, it, i, i? can it, can it, i, i contract antique supper over atomic fall or nuclear winter? this machine, this, me, i, i, it are, is disextinguishable, now & then or forever when, where the very sea-ropes of this ancient dimension come tangled up STUCK RUNNING down brown trunk? eating percolations of vaultanic general coffers

under sog of sagging mudbanks faking under exposed magma, i, i, it, it am succumbing, can expose no matter, see no glint or glimmer of primium substance or dome of FRUIT MANTRA or labour-desert or dense vintage or court of future semantic chugging, only disintegrating furniture unending, seminating the primed-out mud-legs pressing

elastic shoes into the gummy invention... IS FAKE, IS FORGED! i, i, this i, just i, i, am a prisoner on this ship, as are all the others, daily injected with strange liquors, toxic potions running thru us, commandeering our strength, consuming, compelling us

to do what? every day a different task, a new threat. yet nothing changes, ALL REMAINS. the sun is entombed somewhere below, i know, burning things, creating things, tales of excess, tales of deprivation. heart

pounds after a pint & a shot & a caffeine blast & a frantic dance & we realize crawling thru the red-brown slime in our DISINTIGRATING SHIP, that we, this i, this we, are also always decaying

from the inside. this compulsive eating & RELENTLESS INJECTION schedule does never extend our lives nether enlarge our corporeal borders nither expand temporal habitats but contracts our vessels, our vessels

decaying thru many a cautious passage, safety plugs in but BLEEDING THRU unseen cracks. & the drugs! they pump us with excruciating pneumatic animal spirit, bloat our wiz dome, enhance

our ocular pupils, swell our vital motors with outrageous FUEL, SPAWNING this onward impulse traject. sequestered

in rank oblivion fringe, we count biotic ounces in the fish-impounded photoclimb, sinking in thick audio mesh, drowning in saturate sonic thot scavenging inebriate VERBAL PASTE wasted in word-thick articulate ocean picking at trick-knots ripping open this trap-riddled circular org. yoked

to ark-engine artefact, our own fruit-lab under digital locke hoisted & what promised plunder to capture? we do not enter, but wander, die for lack of breath we wander & die, the unnamed we wanders EYELESS UNDER DICTATION, armless, mindless, headless zombie invasion, hauling defunct spirit engine. are wired to machines & compelled to track things, kept alive by plazmik injection. i, i, it, am

zombie crewmember of the PLAZMUD, A HAEMOGLOBIC GENERATION vessel transporting thru oily channels, delivering iron ox to many wayout stations, to strange blue-red capillary fringes under watch of harsh general in red hardhat. eyes alight, he pries open my force-fed mind-shaft, shows me raw waste power. he likes to say we are at the outskirts

of creation, bioengineered to eat solid chunks in arid reactor & generate thru muscular reaction generous donatations to this FLOATING PHARMACEUTICAL distillery. he flicks a switch & we dance with greater urgency. with greater urgency i do & so do you because you are here too, with us & one of us & one with us, whatever. we capture

trapped gasses & feed raw power to corporate grid, open sewers & pit latrines, pump high volumes of solid MATTER, PUMP energy into the airless circuit, produce charged sludge, active paste archetype. & he, general motors, takes us athwart & shows us the navigation panel, an assemblage made of bug-parts & techno-debris, here a bee-brain, there an electric transmitter, receiver, all interlinked

in myriad biomechanical chains. he pinches a rubber thorax & mechanical squeals leak out as thick ORANGE JUICE exudes & an overhead monitor turns pink, casing & display both, & little blue characters appear on screen & your nose begins

to itch as a glare burns your pupils. you shut your eyes & see a polymorphous purple SPOT WITH lining. *that is the island of our destination*, he says. a landfill from before the searise? we each take an unwanted dose

of orange toxic & he takes us below, to avoid a protozoan lion or tiger, escaped from our on-board zoo, he tells us, & shows us the ship's engine. it runs on RED FLUID FLOWING from a trough into a reservoir. alcohol. he is concerned, keeps asking if we are bleeding, *no not now captain*, but soon i am bleeding & so are you & the music turns

dark & foreboding like on a tv drama when something bad is happening but nobody is paying attention & the surgeon general is drunk & does not notice the blood because it is the same red shade as the alcohol fuel pouring INTO THE BIG ENGINE from another trough & in the reservoir together mixing. dark & foreboding music stops, maybe meaning death. i see something solid floating

in the mixing zone where the two troughs meet, ice in bigger & bigger bloody chunks. then a single LARGE RED CUBE gets caught in the drain. the engine stops. the bleeding stops. the music

begins again, different from before but still dark & foreboding. *the red fuel changes the composition of the SHIP'S BODY over the course of the trip*, he says, *to meet the requirements of two kinds of water—fresh & salt perhaps -*

it's remarkable, i say, *that they don't make two kinds of boat. o haven't you heard*, he says thru sabre-like teeth, *the universe*

is circular. all is haze over analog locks, all is smudge & scramble. you are the promised plunder, the rich field of extraction. you are the ox-power, the fossilized peat moss, hardening, blackening under the SPENT GENERATIONS. & we are locked, you & i, us, this overworked steam engine, in complex simulation of turbulent condition at the edge of forbidden plasma, a hot, charged demi-gas confined in outrageous magnetic field inside of ornamental antique battery. & if we don't like it we can change the channel, any time we like, he tells us. shot as unthot wad as unbound clot from big engine bang-boom pulsation into one-way systemic addiction, fate-fisted incessant ramification, the valves ARRANGED TO PREVENT return, away, away, compelled into evershrinking rivers, arms ever-stuck with tubes we are fed

continuous with stuff plucked from wasted industrial seascape & HUGE DRILL-TUBES descend & auger in, tear into surrounding ground & twist right into this outrageous riverbed to extract what bitter juice the pulpular substrate offers. sick, spent, injected, prolonged, we look & look along

the length of the branch & leave off the end to take our daily bath in caustic butter. the vanishing vistas spoil our vantage. plopped in the muddle of the rubbled road, they download a large MOUNTAIN INTO OUR THERMOS, allowing several splashes to land in the adjacent cup, with a wobble causing the brownest spill since. we gather all their rags

to sop up the martian mess, each depositing a chunk in its official pocket. my piece is a 30 micron slice with TRAPPED GASSES & all the usual colours. it pulls me away so i say ok. now it wants to put me in its mass-spectrometer & so i hesitate & then

obey. crudely they drop us from the snowmobiling icefield into a harrowed plain, spotting dark rocks atop our lice-coloured peaks. the thinness of the VEGETATION SHEETS beneath confuse us, so together we break off

some pristine meteorites & stick frozen to our secret plan. the weathering that occurs both ages & preserves us as we stroll over the island's tiny football field, keeping an electronic EYE OUT for stray tackles & ends. when he hollers, they all come

  over, jumping up & down on the warpage & upsetting our systemic pulsation. we see whole days get caught up in the DISCIPLINARY BREEZES & gust away, sometimes two week chunks crashing into & collapsing the surrounding fences & smashing into dust. our doublewalled outents flapping like wings in windtunnels & all our samples

  turn out far-fetched, swimming in & out of the evolving boundaries of our loose eclection. & did it speak about the needles? injections, yes, but MOSTLY EXTRACTIONS, as the descending tubes suck up so much money submerged in analog solution, so the voracious admirals drink your juice, swallow your dissolved oxpower & now

  the PAGE WE WERE ON is gone, so this leg of the cavernous river will end dead. & where we all upend might become the night to end all days. no shit, the fake general drops over once again, unwanted, drunk & dripping & demanding

  we get on his tragic subway. so on we get, packing in & porn thru cargo doors, all rubber gloves & elbows & assholes, hips & bumping in the crowded cars. *enjoy the ride*, he says, trying to betwinkle his dead-jewel eye. the SUBMARINE SMOKES off, segments

  in tow, miles long, all crowded & bodies bumping, jostling, stacked & piling, farts & sweating, entering a tunnel, fast & chugging. & all is dark & damp, green & dripping, seconds stalk upon vanishing seconds, the TWISTING SENTENCE swallowing all, until the train itself also vanishes & we find ourselves inside a cave of many chambers, still moving, still packed & sweating, crowded & shitting, bumping & belching, & the dead GENERAL ACTING as demonic tour-guide drags us thru from room to sweaty room mumbling on about shit transmitting

across generations, pointing out secret places, oozing chambers, lions guarding various trashy treasures, hollowing cluttered halls, decorating muddy walls, clearing out old rubbish, building new stations, PASSAGES, MELTING metals, pounding out the furniture for infinite tracks stretching

across vast minutes of earth. & the temperature begins to drop. it drops & drops like a red ice cube into a thermos full of FREEZING PASTE, the rumbling crowd slowing down, calming down, the walls still moving, still moving, still moving, still. & the temperature

drops further still as the walls of the cave turn from grey & rocky to pink & fleshy, glowing phosphorescent, flashy. the chambers heave & we are compelled to form twin life-lines to CHANNEL HEAT, lining up our bodies, two abreast, in airseat invents raising reasons for test-tasting adjective outthrow, one behind another, untangling & doublefiling, forming twin heatlines, lifelines

across the fleshchambers, exchanging tiny packets of ox-power ACROSS TRANSMISSION CHANNELS. & all at once the walls are speeding, fleshly pinkwalls backward rushing, blurring, blushing past

our filed lines. & tho the pairs are constantly breaking, the powerlines are continuously reforming, until all becomes a blur & all resistance is lost & a bright yellow flash appears at the end & all is rush & blush & flush & fail & fall & laugh... & laugh!?

& laugh! & laugh! & laugh! haha! revert! revert! hoohoo! hoohoo! revert hehe the sure-shelf black-log back along its corroded blurr-path. thwapping gloom-puddle bubble-plunk politely blotted asswipe ascension afterbath, as unmuzzle discharge. as mud. unlock. unclock. unkant. hoho-hahah! hoho-hahah! & drum down dumb dread DOWN IN GUMBO go ground go grunt go nozzle up a truffle, ho-ho, hm-hmmm, ho-ho, hm-hmmm. touch smock hosts mock fistloads of hot cones but tingling softpots goop piling mustard sumpits summering up & slobbered

in what? teaweed? seameat? crement? kongcrete? wrong! hoho-hahah! hoho-hahah! the rubbed up gunk is just swimming in ox-grease! simply glimmering with GLAM-SHAKES pumped off everflowing pissed-off mudded sumpits stuffed with digital dead-sun shreds, hu-huuuh, hu-huuuh, glossing over ghost-dress

in bested-off pretasted stewage middles thickening, hu-huuuh, hu-ha! hoho, hahah! & streaming wendsdays roll right up-mud of ox-battered bonanza baking extra message spun off excess wet jets! hoho, hoohoo! hoho, hahah! message reddening rictus intense insense screaming ruddy labial reading meaning mudded glottle puzzle pulling PALATIAL OUTBREAK feeding, hoho–hahah! & even after eventual airthing ends up evening up momentous art-ark, come dirt of air, come worth of earth, even earthick amplitude hours open up events word eating, oven wheated eden in ore-seat invents risen raisins for test-toasting convectious leftoffer or flavoured floatsum or forged-rotten eggpaste! & all is deny, deny, deny the searing ship-shape ascending asteroid artfact project, ha! weltering in its transatlantic DISCORPORATE BREEZES, please, your stalls are stinking up all cureageous resister, ho! barbing over every reblurbic vector lit up in the null-noting remorphant (hehe!) oxwiper. pluctus fuctus rectus dumptus. us,

us, it, this mobile domestic OX-HERD dragging your galactic piss-tanks & junk-fueled treasure chest across the crumbling retail chains. to raid the retarded commercial spaces & build your hoard of collectable feces? makes us laugh & louder laugh, like we're sinking, hehe! or sing like we're falling, hehe! hehe! laugh like we're sinking

to the BOTTOM OF THE SEA, hehe! fuck off

oxygone lung-killer, BLUE WHALE IN THE BLOOD sucking raw luck like a cut in the back or a bloody taxbreak attack, fuck that. fuck off

zero-in-the-bone existential void, corrupt continuum, general this & general that, decartesian plane, frail imp of errorthrottillian cantegory crashing in our fragrant ground zero habitat, fuck that. fuck off big killer zoom zoom ENGINE, SUCK-math spouting poison pinecones like a careful king flaunting

his radioactive noodle, flogging his favourite junior. & fuck right off zoon, ancient snoozer, hungry skyfisher, lazy mooching newsworthy schmoozer, lousy lump of literate lionshit, hooks hanging from glass towers, lures lowered from iron TOWERCRANES, BITS of human reeled up to your kettle cooking cannibal sky-feast, even where eventual airthing ends evening up momentous earth-ark, fuck!

off! stony vegetable math cooker, sprouting arms that punch thru minds like white death retarding the spark of thot like a slow rot, like a STUCK CLOCK, cluck of a bad luck bird beturding the living word. fuck off

& die rich, Zeen, feeble toxic sneezer, junior patriarch, tiny dictator worm, ambitious ass stuck in the unfinished grass, tiny mind thawing in the frigid backward wind, your inverted winter is forever, but thank heaven i'm elsewhere. fuck off

onion-peel inhabitant, creator of murk, of mud, we love the MUD AS WE LOVE our onion, but not stuck as a death sauce fixed in a check-list as you would have it! fuck off toxic tongue peeler, first & second turd of pigoen-shit deadword, bird of banning bing bang bloom of cosmic juice. fuck off empty powertower, wasting draining bankrupt burnhouse. fuck off shake & BAKE DUST kingdom, paralysis stun hazard, remote control autobot robo-living. fuck off

time vacuum, banality probe, abnormality hunter, bigfuck life-stomper. fuck off immutable cartoon screeches at flesh ears, advertising bomb skid travel, lethargic colourphony moving picture-clocker, sloshing knee-deep in torpid hair-shit. fuck off COSMIC SWEAT stainremover, drabfrantic capitalist winter, rash accidental massacres. fuck off ancient horseshit resurrector in all your stupidstitious professional phases. & what is this

faint whistle that rides the aromatic ORAL WAVES like a foam-coasting ocean flower? tis the death-dreams of an old crow whose lost his caws. tis the soul of an expired moment, a single strata of background radiation from an ancient explosion. go fuck. thus enlighted & enlarged, we carry the still-usable remnants of our portable ark-engine & ox-hoard, follow the TRASH RIVER north to an abandoned strip mall, where soth comes tosh comes tush comes shut comes shot comes shout, scrape a hole in the cluttered bank & watch it slowly fill with black ink mingled with brown sand. we fire

up & boil away the brown shit, smear a sample of black gum over the cracks in our burnt box. further up & further in, arrive at a VAST PLAZA, immense towering banks, looming rust-poles, flickering light-sticks, icy stages, thick black tar oozing at every pore, underlaid

by great overlapping dykes of disintegrating limestone, embedded with myriaded glass splinters, crowned with metallic trees trying to SCRATCH FRESH shapes off the bewildered brown sky. see giant brick-laid escarpments, everywhere streaked with oozing oil, & at last come to an old TAR-SMELLING SHIP & this we board & take control. that was now & this

is then, this, it, i, i, us, alive on this rotten earthly sailing vessel, alive on this time we pulled a globe of premorphous pulp out of the dissolved scrample in our arkaic flash-drive time-capsule & TORE A FRESH STRIP on which to write this script, these five oily books. & we selected a scarred relic, a little pool of clotted waters

from our box of jumbled oily objects & inserted it into our electronic TOMB MACHINE, conjuring strange but familiar spirits. we passed & pre-sent up our temporary tents, nod now, loosen heads, knowing every beat, every scrap, every squirt of lost sonic juice, wondering how to insert ourselves into this epoch-stretched commodious

An electro-luminescent discharge caused by ionization of air under thunder. Referred to as fire but plasma in fact.

dream, how to penetrate the alien object, capture the promised plunder, VALUE SUNKEN in systemic molecular collision. as our anxious eggbeater turns the cut of earth

beyond its worth, dissolves the yolk of ore in magmatic dillusions, we sit in our chaotic time-ravel & stare. ecstatic chainsaw rigor cuts us up red alarms, animates our blue limbs as the RED WHALE in the blood jacks up & we open again the digital sepultura, escape to the void, & yaweh's rightous rage flows

over as we enlarge again & collect again & get lost again & our breath & blood flows into the vast pacific matrix to be one with EXPANDING PLASTIC VORTEX, we assume outrageous identity & all collapses, the metallic disc dissolves. frantic, we scramble

to recover the rabid radio ghost but our ark is already corrupted, dims down, crusts over, is dead crate, lifeforce no longer. search the riverbanks for symptoms of ore, for SPOTS OF BLACK INK, any handle, any detail our indexers can grab hold of, but there is nothing. the manic movement is capitulated. be with us always, WRATHFUL GHOST of electric yahweh, feed us forks of thick red meat, send your burnt offerings up to us & inject us with ferocious rabies, for us, your battery-bled soldiers

of chaos. rejoice! the burnt spear, it roars over us again & again we become one with furious fuel, our blood thickens, blackens, & we are cruel, crude consumed. thus enflamed, we reach into the metallic hoard, we lick, we dip our IRON TONGUES

into the deep-earth plazma, weave, wail, muck about, worming up our destinations with the softwords of our waterlips, MUD AS WHALE, enough! we've been wading all dies irae & our parashoes are still in fasten, tight-tied & unflapping, bodies landing

unfallen. creeping crap, we're nearly near! elmo's flaming dare, his banking glare. & all the tall kings are his tree's barkings. but the bellows are still whispering all our ears to the windings shore. ashore! where its swarming all our visitorcalls. unlock! unkant! shed the remembered entrails of dead generals! recover! rediscover the salting hour, crossing delight in bracing hands, the swollen wade enjoins the waterworms in their moist underweather. STILL THIRSTING after

a lost venture? water your dunes! the nonnews that deserts ever followsumpers thru the shallowest sand-sinks or drowns the lastlight off horse-battered bonanza is hardly a behindtrail worth trialling. the SMELLING HEIGHTS we offer

at the centuring cruise error more than halves the sleeping dues of our nuance, the slowing sights so thorough, so secure against the deeper borrowers, so solid

Our flash drive, the actual ark thru which this trail of industrial message was hauled & loaded in & out of so many plasma-soaked dataplanets.

against the aching brokers, so spiny against the bindless bookers, it's all you know in ILLEGIBLE SECRETS feeling out of the underseizing mounds

of their vulcations. so as the sleeping flags flutter & flatter & the overhead weatherwheels thump & thunder, we at the crust of our CRUMBLING ERROR slip you a sleek wish whenever their look is loosened: a smoothsail around the bond voyages & may your paddle handle the wiz of all the moistest domains these sogging fingerbeasts can flick or fling. wave, wave, thru spastic genesistical storm & captus revelating tempest traptus & the trickle

rips us into forbidden onion launch, zips us up the freefloating bluechannels, kicks us down the four-horse motor &

river rams us ripe thru every ICTUS RAPTUS CAPTUM SPAZUM amendment as we flash out of deadmouth & the rotten temple

collapses. at last, illuminated DROPS SPELL OUT beneath our twisting sweetlamp. our generatrix coasts up to the vertex of its soaking

seed-trail, the delicious aural-fruits just popping out for the big juicing. a luscious unisexual central jazz axis encumbers all before us, stadiumfulls of spermiferous rock & roll conifers overlap with scaly spiral-arranged sporophyllic cyads & our pollen-beaten sacs SPRAWL OUT, NAKED in the ovules. at the fovea centralis, club mosses, spiked horse-power, junk orchestras, punk mosses, clusters of hip-hop. & the dense

retinal photoreceptors concentrate across their encompassing dayglo arenas. & vividly marked conidaen gastropods mollusk out of the subtropics to SHELL

OUT eye-popping stings. & the scoriaen artillary crawl out of their crater, calculating the viscus directrix of their volcanic trajectories. & this is only
 the beginning! fill your drink? then repop the shrink-warped pallet of decapped battles, seaman! the mismatched SIDES ARE SPLITTING wider by the minus, miniature mufflers stuff all this shovel backup downer. & that's all out where indexpensible juiceprocessors aren't over halves for showers! to overlook
 this chuckling boulder, seize chance, charge & change. order that in necessary knots, shrunken general. umbrellas open again, go in, ensign. the showstoppers plug up high praises, UNCORK BATTLES, the whine's high pitch eases out of cellars, dry
 as drain. retires spit spray at all recyclers, peddling away their PASSAGES, KINKS in chains, remove all lids before dropping off, go gutter, seller. no glottle stops here, captain! peeling back
 from the essentials of flood, we pull out our key pronunciations. full-bellied shells will shelter our machines from honeycombs of golden bile until our stockpile of vagrant splinters has eclipsed the colour flaking off of our ROTTING VESSEL. to draw out
 the unabridged barrel-chamber, to breech-load our spent flavours underneath the centrifugal dryer & furthermore textend our precious promise-passage, we obtain CHEMICAL ACTION, mathemodically
  distilling the vascular root-functions with our IMPROVIZING MACHINES at every apicultural revision to the path of moist existinktion. slip, slip, slip,

slop, slap, sleep, sleep, sleep, dream, dream a droopy drama, drip, grip, grope, SLIP IN SHIPS amidst the drift of flipping rocks & arid flaps,

a full align, not a core or a course accursed, a dim anchor, a DAMN CURSE these tiny grey shapes. not islands, not an odd sea or even a far sea, but a here sea, a near sea, a mere sea. then annex

the lower cellar, dweller! we promise the BOTTOM OF THIS will be rotten if only the poop peeps out underneath. what's the name of the hole beneath ships where shit leaves?

Association of Musical Marxists

The ASSOCIATION OF MUSICAL MARXISTS was founded by Andy Wilson and Ben Watson after being subjected to a thirty-minute eternity of Bourdieu-style 'objective' sociology of music at the recent *Historical Materialism* conference.

Sick of being treated like party-spoilers, soppy mystics and 'undertheorised' unprofitable scum, the devotees of truth in music have decided to stand up and make themselves heard.

> WE are no longer going to sit on our hands and bite our tongues
> WE are going to proclaim our proclivities as the cosmo-biologico-social necessity they truly are
> WE are no longer prepared to tolerate boring music and lying hacks 'for the good of the cause'
> WE shall embrace great music regardless of genre as the pattern for reshaping humanity and the key to the dialectic
> For US, music is a test of you and everything about you, and if you fail that test YOU ARE THE ENEMY!!!

We are no longer prepared to be herded in a shtetl marked Art or Noise or *Avant-garde*: we are talking about music, the last location of 'soul' in modern man, the royal road to a satisfied subject and an engaged species being. Our first requirement for anything we take on board is that it's **REVOLUTIONARY**. Hence, we loved to hear Tony Cliff harangue the throng. And we love to read *Society of the Spectacle* – however 'contradictory' that sounds to the accountants of political reason. But how come Cliff professed himself 'deaf' to music? Worse, why did Guy Debord never make public his enthusiasm for the music of John Coltrane and Archie Shepp? For us, late 'Trane is a **PLAN OF ACTION, A PRINCIPLE OF LIFE** and a **CRITICISM OF BUSINESS AS USUAL**. We leave the candyass professionals of music commentary to stew in their own duplicitous juices: we shall take the burning zeal instigated in us by Iancu Dumitrescu and Ana-Maria Avram and use it to revive a tired Marxism, make new friends, create disorder on the streets and bring down the ConDem government. Come and talk to us where you see the **AMM** banner.

xi-2010
info@ammarxists.org
unkant.com

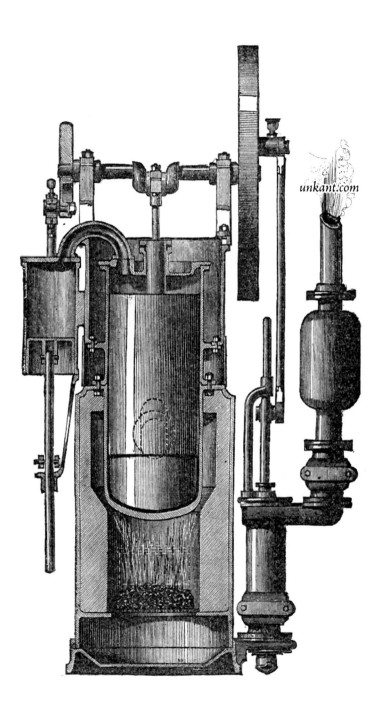

More Years for the Locust
Jim Higgins
ISBN: 978-0-9568176-3-1
Published: Jun 2012, 330pp

"There is a human scale to the story so often missing in the more staid accounts of the left and its history which often create an artificial barrier between readers and the activists being written about, who were after all, people much like them. This dimension of the book which, to put it bluntly, makes it such a good laugh, also provides a great store of what Aristotle would have called practical wisdom. The laughter and the nous are here very closely related and impossible to summarise, they must be read...

The trouble with Higgins is ultimately our own trouble. The reward for recognising this is to be able to rehabilitate and nourish a part of ourselves. The IS tradition is broader than the latest line or missive from the latest CC. This may seem a problem to some but it ought to be seen as a great resource. Revolutionaries too have traditions. Perhaps we are now in a position to learn from Higgins even if we were sadly a bit too stupid to do so before."

John Game, *Foreword*

Blake in Cambridge
Ben Watson
ISBN: 978-0-9568176-8-6
Published: Apr 2012, 168pp

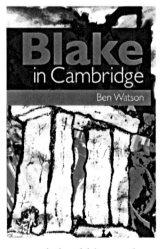

Blake in Cambridge was written after reading William Blake's visionary epic *Milton* during extended bouts of childcare in Coram's Fields in the summer of 2010. *Blake in Cambridge* is the Marxist critique of Eng. Lit. Christopher Caudwell was meant to write, but screwed up due to a CPGB sociology which denies literature the chance to answer back. In Marx's polemic, the jokes of *Tristram Shandy* and *Don Quixote* became weapons in class struggle. This, argues Watson, is how Blake can and should be used.

The **Association of Musical Marxists** says: A revolutionary party would not be paranoid about its members' proclivities. It would not try, like the Lindsey German-era SWP, to insulate members from avant garde extremes and bathe them, infant Cleopatras, in a dilute milk of inoffensive, politically-correct culture – soggy crumbs from the bosses' table. We need to pierce the veil of moralism and fear which protects the bourgeois racket. Blake for the masses! Start here...

1839: The Chartist Insurrection

Dave Black and Chris Ford
ISBN: 978-0-9568176-6-2
Published: Apr 2012, 268pp

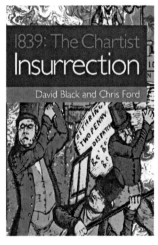

"With its meticulous attention to detailed sources, its comprehensive scope and its exacting research, this book doesn't just address the neglect of this important and interesting episode in Labour movement history, but more importantly it also challenges us to think again about the revolutionary potential of the British Labour movement."

John McDonnell MP, **Foreword**

In retrieving the suppressed history of the Chartist insurrection, David Black and Chris Ford have written a revolutionary handbook. Without romanticism or condescension, they track the difficulties of unifying local revolts without selling out to the 'representative politics' favoured in the parliamentary charade. As today's anti-capitalism faces the problem of anger without organisation, the lessons of the Chartists become crucial. Dialectics is not something to be derived from pure philosophy: by looking at the political problems of an insurgent working class, Black and Ford resurrect the true One-to-Many dialectic.

Association of Musical Marxists

The Struggle for Hearts and Minds: Essays on the Second World War
Ray Challinor
ISBN: 978-0-9568176-1-7
Published: Sep 2011, 128pp

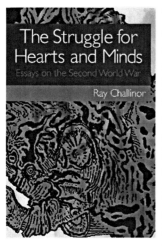

This book of essays is a shocking read, but the shocks arrive from the history itself, not sensationalist writing. We've been told that the Second World War was a war against evil waged by the goodhearted and true. The spectre of Hitler and Nazism is invoked every time NATO bombs are aimed at a defenceless country.

In his scathing account of ruling-class fears, plans and allegiances, Ray Challinor shows how much their every move was governed by competition and self-interest – and anxieties about popular reaction. His evidence shatters the comforting national myth which has been spun around the cataclysm – and shows that people, working-class people, do not like killing each other, they had to be cajoled and manipulated into doing so.

"*Read Ray Challinor's,* The Struggle for Hearts and Minds, *to learn the truth, not just about the Second World War, but of the eternal truth about war: They were bombing Iraqi villages in 1923.*"
Sharon Borthwick, **Unkant**

Happiness: Poems After Rimbaud
Sean Bonney
ISBN: 978-0-9568176-6-2
Published: Sep 2011, 128pp

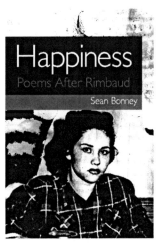

It is impossible to fully grasp Rimbaud's work, and especially *Une Saison en Enfer*, if you have not studied through and understood the whole of Marx's *Capital*. And this is why no English speaking poet has ever understood Rimbaud. Poetry is stupid, but then again, stupidity is not the absence of intellectual ability but rather the scar of its mutilation.

Rimbaud hammered out his poetic programme in 1871, just as the Paris Commune was being blown off the map. He wanted to be there. It's all he talked about. The *"systematic derangement of the senses"* is the social senses, ok, and the *"I"* becomes an *"other"* as in the transformation of the individual into the collective when it all kicks off. It's only in the English speaking world you have to point simple shit like that out. But then again, these poems have **NOTHING TO DO WITH RIMBAUD**. If you think they're translations you're an idiot. In the enemy language it is necessary to lie.

Adorno for Revolutionaries

Ben Watson
ISBN: 978-0-9568176-0-0
Published: May 2011, 256pp

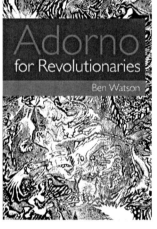

Starting with the commodity form (rather than the 'spirit' lauded by everyone from Classic FM retards to NME journalists), Adorno outlined a revolutionary musicology, a passageway between subjective feeling and objective conditions. In *Adorno for Revolutionaries*, Ben Watson argues that this is what everyone's been looking for since the PCF blackened the name of Marxism by wrecking the hopes of May '68. Batting aside postmodern prattlers and candyass pundits alike, this collection detonates the explosive core of Adorno's thought.

The **Association of Musical Marxists** says: Those 'socialists' who are frightened of their feelings can go stew in their imaginary bookshop. For us, great music is a necessity. To talk about it is to criticize everything that exists.

"For those who have the ears to hear I strongly recommend Adorno For Revolutionaries *as a substantial and very readable effort."*
Dave Black, **Hobgoblin**